HR

INTERVIEW QUESTIONS
YOU'LL MOST LIKELY BE ASKED

225
Interview Questions

VIBRANT
PUBLISHERS

HR
INTERVIEW QUESTIONS
YOU'LL MOST LIKELY BE ASKED

© 2021, By Vibrant Publishers, USA. All rights reserved. No part of this publication may be reproduced or distributed in any form or by any means, or stored in a database or retrieval system, without the prior permission of the publisher.

Paperback ISBN 10 :   1-949395-96-0
Paperback ISBN 13 :   978-1-949395-96-9
Ebook ISBN 10:   1-949395-75-8
Ebook ISBN 13:   978-1-949395-75-4

Library of Congress Control Number: 2018904084

This publication is designed to provide accurate and authoritative information in regard to the subject matter covered. The Author has made every effort in the preparation of this book to ensure the accuracy of the information. However, information in this book is sold without warranty either expressed or implied. The Author or the Publisher will not be liable for any damages caused or alleged to be caused either directly or indirectly by this book.

Vibrant Publishers books are available at special quantity discount for sales promotions, or for use in corporate training programs. For more information please write to **bulkorders@vibrantpublishers.com**

Please email feedback / corrections (technical, grammatical or spelling) to **spellerrors@vibrantpublishers.com**

To access the complete catalogue of Vibrant Publishers, visit www.vibrantpublishers.com

5-Star Review by Readers' Favorite

If you are job hunting, you will face the dreaded job interview. Many fear the interview because they are unsure how to answer the questions. Reading HR Interview Questions You'll Most Likely Be Asked by Vibrant Publishers is a fantastic way to prepare for the best job interview ever. Two-hundred-twenty-five of the most often asked interview questions make this book invaluable. All the questions have suggested answers and why the answers matter. Many of them contain concrete examples. Remember to stay positive with your answers. Yes, one of the most popular interview questions deals with your weakness. Be able to show you know how to prioritize the issues. You are valuable and would be a great addition to any company. The key is to sell yourself and your value to the interviewer.

Job interviews are not something most people go to often. As a result, there is an inherent fear of the interview. Vibrant Publishers wants to relieve the stress connected with interviewing for a job. HR Interview Questions You'll Most Likely Be Asked will help you prepare for your interview no matter what your career choice. Interviewers look for your stand on ethics. Be sure to clearly explain your view of ethics and how they affect your work ethic. A common question has to do with comparing yourself to an animal. This is not about the animal's traits but your ability to think outside the box. Remember not only to answer the questions but to give your reasoning. Reading this book prepares you to ace any job interview.

This review is for an earlier edition.

This page is intentionally left blank

Table of Contents

Chapter 1	Creativity	7
Chapter 2	Leadership	15
Chapter 3	Teamwork	41
Chapter 4	Deadlines and Time Management	53
Chapter 5	Dedication and Attitude	65
Chapter 6	Personality	73
Chapter 7	Decision Making	95
Chapter 8	Goals	107
Chapter 9	Creative Questions	117
Chapter 10	Customer Service	131
Chapter 11	Background and Experience	139
Chapter 12	Business Skills and Knowledge	153
Chapter 13	Communication	163

Chapter **14** Job Searching and Scheduling   173

Chapter **15** Knowledge of the Company   187

        Index   196

Dear Reader,

Thank you for purchasing **HR Interview Questions You'll Most Likely Be Asked.**

Review these typical interview questions and think about how you would answer them. Read the answers listed; you will find best possible answers along with strategy suggestions.

We are committed to publishing books that are content-rich, concise and approachable enabling more readers to read and make the fullest use of them. We hope this book provides the most enriching learning experience as you prepare for your interview.

Should you have any questions or suggestions, feel free to email us at
reachus@vibrantpublishers.com

Thanks again for your purchase. Good luck with your interview!

– Vibrant Publishers Team

facebook.com/vibrantpublishers

About the Author

Pamela Ellsworth is a PHR certified HR consultant with over 10 years in the field. She has studied and trained on psychology, sociology, behavior modification, motivational interviewing, and more. Her career has taken her from working in state prisons, to small businesses, and government agencies. While she has extensive experience in all facets of human resources including employee relations, benefits, retirement, leave administration workers compensation and safety, her forte and passion is in recruitment and selection, on-boarding, and coaching.

She has screened thousands of resumes and applications, conducted hundreds of interviews, and hired many excited new employees. She loves motivating people to be their best and offers coaching on how to walk into any interview with confidence and handle any question the interview panel throws at them with ease. She consults businesses on their recruitment and selection programs and policy issues. In her free time Pamela is active in children's ministries and community outreach.

1

Creativity

Leadership

Teamwork

Deadlines and Time Management

Dedication and Attitude

Personality

Decision Making

Goals

Creative Questions

Customer Service

Background and Experience

Business Skills and Knowledge

Communication

Job Searching and Scheduling

Knowledge of the Company

001. Every business faces problems that affect productivity and profitability. Can you share with me a solution you developed for a workplace problem that was unusual or unexpected, and actually led to increased productivity or profitability?

Answer:

The correct answer will provide quantifiable evidence of the candidate's efforts which increased profitability and productivity.

As an example:

A customer placed a large order for an item with specifications that were significantly different from the product offered by my company. I needed to meet this customer's needs without creating increased production costs. To satisfy this customer, I worked with company engineers and found a way to modify the production machinery to meet this need without increasing my company's production costs. As part of the engineering process, I was able to implement cost savings through reduced labor costs and better utilization of the required raw materials.

---

002. Can you describe how you analyzed a workplace problem you have faced, and how your analysis led to the solution?

Answer:

The correct answer should provide evidence of the candidate's analytical skills, and the candidate's ability to look at an issue from different angles and develop the best solution to a problem.

As an example:

The employer wanted to ramp up production to three shifts per day to meet increased demand for a product without hiring more than five new employees. I found a way to rearrange the existing employees' schedules without creating significant dissatisfaction. Additionally; I was able to fit the five new employees into the schedule in such a way that they were able to work smoothly together to increase the production.'

003. There are times when customers are unhappy with your company's product or service and expect a solution that is more than what is normally provided. Can you share a time when you were able to provide a solution to an unusual customer expectation that made both customer and management happy?

Answer:

The correct answer should provide insight into the candidate's attitudes towards meeting customer service challenges. The answer should provide evidence of the candidate's willingness to creatively respond to difficult customers without violating company policies.

As an example:

An important customer from a different time zone had a need to regularly conduct business outside of my company's normal business hours. I found a way to make a customer service representative available without increasing over time hours. I was able to meet the customer's needs without increasing the financial burden on the company.

004. Describe workplace innovations you have developed on your own initiative.

Answer:

The correct answer should provide tangible evidence of the candidate's willingness to take the initiative to solve problems without being prompted by supervisors.

As an example:

My company recorded employee time on paper time cards, and to reduce payroll expenses. I initiated a project to launch fully computerized system. It included reporting payroll taxes and fees to the state and federal governments, and a direct deposit system for the payment of employee salaries. My efforts saved the company thousands of dollars each year in tracking and paying payroll expenses.

005. Describe workplace innovations you helped develop as a member of a team.

Answer:

The correct response to this question will show how the candidate is able to work as a team member.

As an example:

I was assigned to a management team with the task of developing an entire new line of interior paint products that included new colors, new textures and competitive retail pricing. I was able to help the team develop a customer survey that when completed showed the team exactly which products customers would desire and would purchase if priced right.

006. Where do you find ideas?

Answer:

Ideas can come from all places, and an interviewer wants to see that your ideas are just as varied. Mention multiple places that you gain ideas from, or settings in which you find yourself brainstorming. Additionally, elaborate on how you record ideas or expand upon them later.

As an example:

I am constantly taking notes on a notepad or in my phone throughout the day of things I would like to revisit later. I get ideas during work meetings, listening to my coworkers struggles and updates, take notes and research later how we can improve workflow. I will also get ideas via my network when they put out new innovative things they are pursuing in their workplace, I will see how I may be able to apply those innovations in my own company.

007. How do you achieve creativity in the workplace?

Answer:

It's important to show the interviewer that you're capable of being resourceful and innovative in the workplace, without stepping outside the lines of company values. Explain where ideas normally stem from for you (examples may include an exercise such as list-making or a mind map), and connect this to a particular task in your job that it would be helpful to be creative in.

As an example:

I was assigned to a safety and wellness taskforce. Most people were walking on their breaks anyway, just not together. I signed up for a three month hosted walking challenge in which people could still walk on their own on their breaks, however, they were encouraged to interact with their coworkers and engage in some healthy competition in tracking their progress. This ended up getting more people to get up and exercise while also building morale and a sense of teamwork.

008. How do you push others to create ideas?

Answer:

If you're in a supervisory position, this may be requiring employees to submit a particular number of ideas, or to complete regular idea-generating exercises, in order to work their creative muscles. However, you can also push others around you to create ideas simply by creating more of your own. Additionally, discuss with the interviewer the importance of questioning people as a way to inspire ideas and change.

As an example:

Each staff meeting I encourage staff members to bring a problem or challenge they have been facing or had faced since our last meeting, along with a solution. I also encourage employees to attend regular professional development opportunities whether it is a free webinar, a training, or even read newly published articles in their field, and share things they have learned or trending topics with the team.

009. Describe your creativity.

Answer:
Try to keep this answer within the professional realm, but if you have an impressive background in something creative outside of your employment history, don't be afraid to include it in your answer also. The best answers about creativity will relate problem-solving skills, goal-setting, and finding innovative ways to tackle a project or make a sale in the workplace. However, passions outside of the office are great, too (so long as they don't cut into your work time or mental space).

As an example:
I participate in a volunteer group outside of work who provides meals for homeless people. The company I worked for was seeking connections to the community and ways for the employees to be involved in something bigger than their specific roles at work, so with permission form the company, I hosted a fundraising event put on the company where the employees worked a spaghetti dinner to raise funds for the homeless charity. This boosted employee teamwork and comradery and a sense of purpose amongst them.

This page is intentionally left blank

2

Creativity

Leadership

Teamwork

Deadlines and Time Management

Dedication and Attitude

Personality

Decision Making

Goals

Creative Questions

Customer Service

Background and Experience

Business Skills and Knowledge

Communication

Job Searching and Scheduling

Knowledge of the Company

010. Was there a time you were called upon to reorganize your department? If so, what steps did you take to ensure the reorganization was successful?

Answer:

The candidate should be able to relate to a verifiable time when she was asked to reorganize her department. The correct answer should say something like, "just last year my company decided there should be reorganization program because the internet had significantly changed the way we were doing business."

As an example:

My first step was to identify the exact business functions that were driving the need for change. Secondly, I identified the functions that were working properly and should not be changed. Thirdly, I made a determination of how the people in the department needed to be reassigned to best accomplish the reorganization. In the end, the reorganization was successful, and the company's profits were increased.

011. Tell me about a time when you led a team to successfully complete a project.

Answer:

The correct answer should describe a situation where the candidate was able to act as a project manager of a project with a team involved. It should explain how the candidate analyzed what needed to be done, how they delegated the members of the team and oversaw the project, and what the outcome was.

As an example:

Last year my management team was assigned the task of finding a way to improve our company's overall customer service rating. We were having trouble finding and retaining customer service representatives that were responsive to the needs of our customers. Through customer service surveys and close observation of customer service interactions, we were able to identify a number of customer service representatives that were providing outstanding service to our customers. We assigned these people as trainers and mentors for the purpose of motivating the entire staff to provide a high level of service to our customers.

012. Describe a time when you played a major leadership role in a special event.

Answer:

To answer this question correctly, the candidate should be able to describe an actual event in which she was the primary leader. The special event could be a job fair, awards banquet, marketing meeting or other event.

As an example:

Our Company is constantly looking for talented people. We feel the greatest competitive advantage we have is our people. In April last year, I was given the responsibility to set up a regional job fair designed to attract college graduates. The job fair was a total success. We had over 1000 recent college graduates come to the job fair. Our human resources people were able to fill all of our open positions.

013. How have the people around you responded to your leadership efforts?

Answer:

The expected answer from the candidate is the people he was leading responded very well to his leadership efforts. The candidate should be able to provide solid evidence that people respond to him in a positive manner.

As an example:

For my efforts over the last year to increase my department's sales performance, I received the highest recognition the company provides. The people working in my department responded in an overwhelmingly positive manner to the programs I installed. My department was able to improve sales performance by 15 percent.

014. Describe your strengths as a leader.

Answer:

A good answer to this question would be one where the candidate is able to describe elements of his leadership style that make him a great leader, including what elements people respond well to, how he motivates a team, and his work ethic.

As an example:

One of my greatest strengths as a leader is my ability to motivate people to accomplish tasks they felt were too difficult for them. Recently I worked with a team to overhaul the way we handled incoming shipments. We have many deliveries come in throughout the day, and our efforts to handle the work load were strained to the limit. Working together, we developed a work schedule that maximized the number of people we had available to meet peak workload requirements.

Leadership

015. Describe the greatest weakness in your leadership style.

Answer:
The candidate should answer this question in an honest and open manner. It is hard for some people to admit any weakness, making this question a great indicator of the candidate's willingness to be transparent. Having a solid answer shows the candidate is self aware, and whatever weakness is shared should be immediately followed by how the candidate works on bettering themselves to overcome said weakness.

As an example:
There are times I am not as observant as I should be. While working on a project earlier this year, I failed to see that an important element of the plan had been done incorrectly. My error caused us to miss an important deadline. I am working very hard to improve my observation skills.

016. If a group of people in your department were talking about you behind your back, what do you think they would be saying about you?

Answer:
The candidate may be reluctant to venture and answer for this question, nevertheless the interviewer should press for an answer. This question should shed significant light on the candidate's self-image.

As an example:
I have noticed on occasions that my actions cause some interesting conversations throughout my department. It is hard for me to ignore what is being said. Some people say that I cater to the boss's whims

in an effort to get my name at the top of the promotion list. All I am concerned about is doing the best job that I can. I can't control what other people say about me.

017. Describe a difficult project that required you to build consensus on a divisive issue.

Answer:

Some candidates may consider this a difficult question to answer. Although it is difficult, the interviewer is looking for the candidate to reveal how he deals with divisiveness in the workplace and how he comes up with creative solutions to bring people together for a common good.

As an example:

We had a project to complete that was so large it required the work of three departments. Right in the middle of the project, a serious dispute arose over which department would take the lead position on the project. Tempers became very hot because of the political infighting. Through many hours of painstaking negotiation, I helped everyone involved find a way to put their best foot forward and receive the recognition they were looking for.

018. Describe a project or task that required you to develop agreement or cooperation between departments.

Answer:

The candidate should be able to provide tangible evidence that she is able to work with other leaders to get important work accomplished.

Leadership

As an example:
We had a project to improve the wheel bearings on the tricycles our company sells. My department was in charge of the bearings, and another department was in charge of developing the new wheels that would be used on the tricycle. It took significant interdepartmental cooperation to get the bearings and wheels to the correct size for each model of tricycle the company sold.

019. Describe a situation when you needed to build support within your department for an idea you thought would greatly benefit your company.

Answer:
To answer this question correctly, the candidate should describe a situation which required him to build support for his vision and make his ideas become a reality.

As an example:
I had this idea of finding a way to get the company to develop a child care center in our building. It would be very convenient for people with small children who worked in the building. The initial start-up costs would be significant, but the long-term benefits in increased productivity would pay for the project. It took me almost two years to make my idea become a reality, but everyone in the company is very happy the child care center is in operation.

020. Would you rather receive more authority or more responsibility at work?

Answer:
There are pros and cons to each of these options, and your interviewer will be more interested to see that you can provide

a critical answer to the question. Receiving more authority may mean greater decision-making power and may be great for those with outstanding leadership skills, while greater responsibility may be a growth opportunity for those looking to advance steadily throughout their careers.

As an example:

I would say I am a good example of a "servant leader" in how I work within teams. I have a natural ability to lead and people naturally follow me. I am a natural project manager and can see the big picture as well as minute details. With that said, I listen to what my team says and encourage and value all of their input. It is all about having the ability to lead and make concise and proper decisions, while at the same time taking in to account the opinions and ideas of the entire team and allowing for improving in your decisions when need be.

021. What do you do when someone in a group isn't contributing their fair share?

Answer:

This is a particularly important question if you're interviewing for a position in a supervisory role - explain the ways in which you would identify the problem, and how you would go about pulling aside the individual to discuss their contributions. It's important to understand the process of creating a dialogue, so that you can communicate your expectations clearly to the individual, give them a chance to respond, and to make clear what needs to change. After this, create an action plan with the group member to ensure their contributions are on par with others in the group.

Leadership

As an example:

I would say I am a good example of a "servant leader" in how I work within teams. I have a natural ability to lead and people naturally follow me. I am a natural project manager and can see the big picture as well as minute details. With that said, I listen to what my team says and encourage and value all of their input. It is all about having the ability to lead and make concise and proper decisions, while at the same time taking in to account the opinions and ideas of the entire team and allowing for improving in your decisions when need be.

022. Tell me about a time when you made a decision that was outside of your authority.

Answer:

While an answer to this question may portray you as being decisive and confident, it could also identify you to an employer as a potential problem employee. Instead, it may be best to slightly refocus the question into an example of a time that you took on additional responsibilities, and thus had to make decisions that were outside of your normal authority (but which had been granted to you in the specific instance). Discuss how the weight of the decision affected your decision-making process, and the outcomes of the situation.

As an example:

I had a customer call requesting to have their monthly payment that was already due, waived due to service they felt was subpar. The manager was the only one with the authority to make this decision and was out that day. The customer was very upset and ready to cancel services. I deferred the payment that was due that day and over-rode the automatic cancelation that was set to take place since the customer was behind on payments, and assured the manager was going to contact the customer the next day. When they were able to speak, the customer issue was resolved and they decided to continue our services.

023. Are you comfortable going to supervisors with disputes?

Answer:

If a problem arises, employers want to know that you will handle it in a timely and appropriate manner. Emphasize that you've rarely had disputes with supervisors in the past, but if a situation were to arise, you feel perfectly comfortable in discussing it with the person in question in order to find a resolution that is satisfactory to both parties.

As an example:

I went to my supervisor with some adjustments that needed to be made to a report they had me format and submit to the owner of the company. When I approached the supervisor about their errors they became immediately defensive in nature, until I assured them I just happened to notice the discrepancies in numbers and wanted to bring it to their attention so they could adjust it prior to it being submitted, so he and our department looked good. I assured him that I was looking out for the integrity of the work we produced and wanted to do my best to support him. He thanked me and the report was submitted without errors.

024. If you had been in charge at your last job, what would you have done differently?

Answer:

No matter how many ideas you have about how things could run better, or opinions on the management at your previous

Leadership

job, remain positive when answering this question. It's okay to show thoughtful reflection on how something could be handled in order to increase efficiency or improve sales but be sure to keep all of your suggestions focused on making things better, rather than talking about ways to eliminate waste or negativity.

As an example:

I would have focused on more cross training of the department staff so we would have been able to better assist each other during our own downtime, or in times of an influx of workload or emergency situations in a team member's role or position. This would have helped minimize confusion and back log, allowing for the entire department to be more up to speed and efficient.

025. Do you believe employers should praise or reward employees for a job well done?

Answer:

Recognition is always great after completing a difficult job, but there are many employers who may ask this question as a way to infer as to whether or not you'll be a high-maintenance worker. While you may appreciate rewards or praise, it's important to convey to the interviewer that you don't require accolades to be confident that you've done your job well. If you are interviewing for a supervisory position where you would be the one praising other employees, highlight the importance of praise in boosting team morale.

As an example:

I believe that each employee is different in the way they respond to praise and rewards and if they even desire it. Some may desire it greatly and work toward praise, and some don't like being in the spotlight. It is important to make sure employees are aware they are hired to do a job and are expected to complete their tasks. With that said, employees are human, and have stressful days, outside lives, and at times even just showing up to work and working hard deserves praise in itself. It is important to let employees know they are valued as humans supporting the organization and not just an employee number. Quarterly free employee luncheons for all staff with music and food, and recognition of someone who may have gone above and beyond in an extraordinary circumstance is a great way to keep morale and comradery up.

026. What do you believe is the most important quality a leader can have?

Answer:

There are many important skills for a leader to have in any business, and the most important component of this question is that you explain why the quality you choose to highlight is important. Try to choose a quality such as communication skills, or an ability to inspire people, and relate it to a specific instance in which you displayed the quality among a team of people.

As an example:

Communication is key in leadership. Having the ability to take in to consideration all aspects and every scenario before making a decision, but being able to be the one to ultimately make the decision whether it is going to be popular or not, is something a leader needs to be able to do. The important part is being able to really listen to your employees and hear their concerns out, letting them know you value their opinion, then explain to them why you made the decision that you did. Most times employees just want to feel heard. Having

Leadership

open lines of communication at all times is essential for maintaining trust amongst the staff. I made the decision to adjust our vacation request policy to reflect employees need to request vacation at least two weeks prior to their time off, which was met with much dismay. Once I explained the decision was based upon having overlapping days off, inadequate staffing, unfairness amongst coworkers, and loss of profits and it was going to be better for the company and the employees, they understood.

027. Tell me about a time when an unforeseen problem arose. How did you handle it?

Answer:

It's important that you are resourceful, and level-headed under pressure. An interviewer wants to see that you handle problems systematically, and that you can deal with change in an orderly process. Outline the situation clearly, including all solutions and results of the process you implemented.

As an example:

As the safety officer at my last employer, I had an important two o'clock meeting with department heads that had been on the calendar for a month and could not be moved due to the executive's busy schedules. At the same time, I had an urgent safety issue in the field I needed to run out to. I was split between the two issues so I had my intern take the presentation I had prepared to the meeting, explain the situation, and show the presentation to them anyway. He clarified things he could and took notes on their questions and items he was not equipped to address, and we scheduled a follow up conference call for the next day to go over the pending questions I was not there to answer. We were able to tie up loose ends on the follow up call and move forward with the project the next day. The executives understood the situation I was faced with and appreciated not having to put the project on hold.

028. Can you give me an example of a time when you were able to improve X objective at your previous job?

Answer:

It's important here to focus on an improvement you made that created tangible results for your company. Increasing efficiency is certainly a very important element in business, but employers are also looking for concrete results such as increased sales or cut expenses. Explain your process thoroughly, offering specific numbers and evidence wherever possible, particularly in outlining the results.

As an example:

I was able to successfully reduce the hold time by 4 minutes on each customer call and streamline the wait list process by suggesting a software in which all customer service reps had access to a monitor that showed all customer calls. The monitor displayed how many calls were active, pending, or on hold (and with which rep), and which line they were on. Reps could easily hang up a call, look at the board and see which line needed to be picked up next. This improved workflow for the customer service department, allowed for approximately 20 more customer resolutions per day, increased profits by 30% in terms of new orders that could now come in, and increased customer satisfaction and company ratings.

Leadership

029. Tell me about a time when a supervisor did not provide specific enough direction on a project.

Answer:

While many employers want their employees to follow very specific guidelines without much decision-making power, it's important also to be able to pick up a project with vague direction and to perform self-sufficiently. Give examples of necessary questions that you asked and specify how you determined whether a question was something you needed to ask of a supervisor or whether it was something you could determine on your own.

As an example:

I had a large project already pending when my supervisor was about to leave for vacation. Before her vacation she gave me another project and did not leave deadlines along with it. I analyzed the project and determined it was a new client and I did not want to leave them wondering. I continued with my pending project and made contact with the new client to introduce myself and set up a call to discuss their needs. This bought me time while also allowing me to obtain more information. It was still unclear as to what the deadlines were and it did not seem urgent so I continued with my existing, as well as set aside time each afternoon to begin working on the new client's project as well.

030. Tell me about a time when you were in charge of leading a project.

Answer:

Lead the interviewer through the process of the project, just as you would have with any of your team members. Explain the goal of the project, the necessary steps, and how you delegated tasks to your team. Include the results, and what you learned as a result of the leadership opportunity.

As an example:

As an HR Assistant helping while the HR Benefits Rep was out on leave, I was put in charge of the annual employee benefits open enrollment for a large organization. I spoke with the manager ahead of time to gather as much information as I could on what had worked in the past in terms of timelines and work flow, and added a couple of helpful changes myself such as a filing system for the different benefit changes as they were going to come in. The week prior to the beginning of open enrollment, I had a meeting with the HR department to go over each form and explain to my team how I was going to distribute each form and made helpful cheat sheets of information for them to each keep at their desk in instances of an employee coming with questions and I may be unavailable. The entire process went smoothly and organized, and employees commented on how easy it was.

031. Tell me about a suggestion you made to a former employer that was later implemented.

Answer:

Employers want to see that you're interested in improving your company and doing your part - offer a specific example of something you did to create a positive change in your previous job. Explain how you thought of the idea, how your supervisors received it, and what other employees thought was the idea was put into place.

As an example:

I suggested we start an innovation committee to bring staff together to discuss new ideas they had for the workplace. These ideas included

facebook.com/vibrantpublishers

a wide variety of things such as ways to implement employee recognition, snack machine options, changes to the customer lobby, and anything and everything in between. While not all ideas were acted upon by management, a variation of most of the ideas were implemented. This made the employees feel a sense of ownership and belonging in the company, as well as improved morale and teamwork.

032. Tell me about a time when you thought of a way something in the workplace could be done more efficiently.

Answer:

Focus on the positive aspects of your idea. It's important not to portray your old company or boss negatively, so doesn't elaborate on how inefficient a particular system was. Rather, explain a situation in which you saw an opportunity to increase productivity or to streamline a process, and explain in a general step-by-step how you implemented a better system.

As an example:

Our department had set aside Fridays as "filing days" for paperwork that was collected throughout the week. While this was definitely a great idea, if a coworker called out sick, or we had a large amount of filing in one week, there would be times when we would not get it all done on Friday, or it would be very stressful due to the high volume of paperwork we received throughout the week. I suggested that we started to file throughout the week during our downtime between projects so we would not have a backlog all on one day. I also noticed that the last half hour of each day, some coworkers would start "packing up" and with the work we did, we couldn't really start a new project within the last little bit of time so we would start packing up and then file for the last thirty minutes of each day until it was time to clock out. This greatly reduced the amount we had piled up for Fridays, as well as kept productivity higher throughout the week.

033. Is there a difference between leading and managing people - which is your greater strength?

Answer:

There is a difference - leaders are often great idea people, passionate, charismatic, and with the ability to organize and inspire others, while managers are those who ensure a system runs, facilitate its operations, make authoritative decisions, and who take great responsibility for all aspects from overall success to the finest decisions. Consider which of these is most applicable to the position, and explain how you fit into this role, offering concrete examples of your past experience.

As an example:

I am a good leader because I take time to think about all possible aspects of a project and how it may affect each employee tasked to work on the project. I do my best to see things from each perspective, anticipating and planning things that may go wrong, and focusing on what could go right. I pitch ideas in a way where I am able to garner support from the employees and make them feel they are a part of something great.

034. Do you function better in a leadership role, or as a worker on a team?

Answer:

It is important to consider what qualities the interviewer is looking for in your position, and to express how you embody

Leadership

this role. If you're a leader, highlight your great ideas, drive and passion, and ability to incite others around you to action. If you work great in teams, focus on your dedication to the task at hand, your cooperation and communication skills, and your ability to keep things running smoothly.

As an example:

While I am able to work well in either role, I find that I am better suited for leadership roles since it comes so naturally for me. Even in positions where I was not the boss, I had people coming to me for suggestions, to bounce ideas off of, and looking for support. I am good at project management and fitting the right people in to the right place where their skills and personality, as well as work ethic will be best suited. If I find someone on a team is struggling with keeping up, I am able to find creative ways to include them and change their tasks to something possibly even outside of their comfort zone, where they are better suited to contribute to the team. I find the best quality in each employee and motivate them in to action.

035. Tell me about a time when you discovered something in the workplace that was disrupting your (or others) productivity - what did you do about it.

Answer:

Try to not focus on negative aspects of your previous job too much, but instead choose an instance in which you found a positive, and quick, solution to increase productivity. Focus on the way you noticed the opportunity, how you presented a solution to your supervisor, and then how the change was implemented (most importantly, talk about how you led the change initiative). This is a great opportunity for you to display your problem-solving skills, as well as your resourceful nature and leadership skills.

As an example:

> Our one and only timeclock was continuously met with long lines of all staff clocking out at the same time. This would cause chaos at the clock out line, disgruntled employees, employees in a hurry skipping the process entirely, and employees packing up for the day early so they could "get in line." I suggested we add a second timeclock on the other side of the room near the second entry door to alleviate the line. This helped productivity because employees did not feel the need to pack up early and waste time standing at a timeclock and eased some of the grumpiness felt at the end of the day.

036. How do you perform in a job with clearly-defined objectives and goals?

Answer:

> It is important to consider the position when answering this question - clearly, it is best if you can excel in a job with clearly-defined objectives and goals (particularly if you're in an entry level or sales position). However, if you're applying for a position with a leadership role or creative aspect to it, be sure to focus on the ways that you additionally enjoy the challenges of developing and implementing your own ideas.

As an example:

> I enjoy having a set guideline of rules to abide by. This helps to streamline processes, especially when dealing in customer-centric companies. With that said, if I see a policy that can be improved on, I have no problem with bringing my ideas to the forefront, testing them and if they work, implementing them. With the improvement in a process, the policy would need to be updated, and all employees notified of the new procedures so all staff are on the same page.

facebook.com/vibrantpublishers

Leadership

037. How do you perform in a job where you have great decisionmaking power?

Answer:

The interviewer wants to know that, if hired, you won't be the type of employee who needs constant supervision or who asks for advice, authority, or feedback every step of the way. Explain that you work well in a decisive, productive environment, and that you look forward to taking initiative in your position.

As an example:

I have been given the opportunity to be in the role of decision maker many times in previous roles. There are times where a guideline exists of how to properly perform the job and limitations within your role, however, there are instances where you must make a prompt decision on the spot. During these times I have no problem with being creative in solving a problem and informing my superiors of what took place afterward, to keep them in the loop.

038. If you saw another employee doing something dishonest or unethical, what would you do?

Answer:

In the case of witnessing another employee doing something dishonest, it is always best to act in accordance with company policies for such a situation - and if you don't know what this company's specific policies are, feel free to simply state that you would handle it according to the policy and by reporting it to the appropriate persons in charge. If you are aware of the company's policies (such as if you are seeking a promotion within your own company), it is best to specifically outline your actions according to the policy.

As an example:

> This really depends on what they were doing. Some things such as stealing large amounts of money, equipment, or anything that puts themselves or someone else in danger, would need to be reported immediately. There may be times however, where a coworker is perhaps breaking a policy or going around protocol to save time or cut costs, and it may be detrimental to themselves or the company. In these instances, I would feel comfortable discussing the issue with my coworker myself and seeing if I can help them in any way and let them know that what they were doing was wrong. They may not have even realized it was wrong or may have been going through rough times. If they continued to do so even after we spoke, I would feel comfortable bringing the issue to management.

039. Tell me about a time when you learned something on your own that later helped in your professional life.

Answer:

> This question is important because it allows the interviewer to gain insight into your dedication to learning and advancement. Choose an example solely from your personal life, and provide a brief anecdote ending in the lesson you learned. Then, explain in a clear and thorough manner how this lesson has translated into a usable skill or practice in your position.

As an example:

> I work with a volunteer organization on the weekends. When the president of the organization was unavailable to lead a fundraising event, I had to step in and assure the event went smoothly, set it up, and emcee to the crowd. I was very nervous but this ended up helping increase my public speaking skills drastically, and the next

Leadership

team meeting we had at work I was able to speak to my coworkers and present my project without feeling nervous. I also was asked to coordinate the next employee event at work and used some of the things from the volunteer event I worked at in the employee event at work, such as seating arrangement and check in process. I became a more valued member of the team at work.

040. Tell me about a time when you developed a project idea at work.

Answer:

Choose a project idea that you developed that was typical of projects you might complete in the new position. Outline where your idea came from, the type of research you did to ensure its success and relevancy, steps that were included in the project, and the end results. Offer specific before and after statistics, to show its success.

As an example:

We were having difficulties in hiring new sales staff. I developed the idea to update our sales position job descriptions. The job descriptions we had were outdated and had not been updated in several years, during which time, many new software tools had become available, and the position had changed. The sales team got together and reviewed the current job description and provided their input as to what they felt should be added and removed from the descriptions, then management reviewed and made updates accordingly. Once we began running job ads with the new job description, we had an increase in qualified sales professionals applying who understood the position they applied for and were better matches.

041. Tell me about a time when you took a risk on a project.

Answer:

Whether the risk involved something as complex as taking on a major project with limited resources or time, or simply volunteering for a task that was outside your field of experience, show that you are willing to stretch out of your comfort zone and to try new things. Offer specific examples of why something you did was risky and explain what you learned in the process - or how this prepared you for a job objective you later faced in your career.

As an example:

I worked in the engineering department of a utility company. We had an emergency situation where a water pipe broke in the community and were overwhelmed with customer calls from the community regarding their utility bills. During this time, there were two customer service reps out on leave, so I offered my assistance since I was in between major projects. I was completely out of my comfort zone however I assisted with taking customer calls, answering basic questions, and taking names and numbers of the customers I was unable to help, so the supervisor could call them back later. I was able to collect payment from approximately 100 customers, successfully answer about 50 questions, and take information for call backs on another 25. I learned more about how what I did in my department connected to the customer service reps and the types of questions they are asked by customers and challenges they face. After this situation, our two departments began working together more, and even had quarterly meetings together where we provided updates on items that may directly impact the work of the other department.

042. What would you tell someone who was looking to get into this field?

Answer:
This question allows you to be the expert - and will show the interviewer that you have the knowledge and experience to go along with any training and education on your resume. Offer your knowledge as advice of unexpected things that someone entering the field may encounter and be sure to end with positive advice such as the passion or dedication to the work that is required to truly succeed.

As an example:
If someone were looking to get into the field of sales, I would suggest first looking in to what certificate programs or degree options are available that may help with the field. I would also suggest if you are not comfortable with speaking to others whether one on one or in group settings, to take a public speaking class to boost your confidence. I would suggest learning the ins and outs about sales and finding a product that you are truly passionate about selling. If you are not passionate about your business, especially in sales, you will not do well. Once you find what you are passionate about selling, learn everything you can about it. If it is a product, use it and test it. If it is a service, try it out. Remember to allow yourself time in the beginning to fail a few times, this is not the end of the world as it helps you learn. Keep being persistent in your work and learn what works and does not work with your target audience. Have a positive attitude with customers and clients, find a balance between seeming too pushy or eager, but not too timid and disinterested, and don't forget the follow ups after making first contact!

This page is intentionally left blank

3

Creativity

Leadership

Teamwork

Deadlines and Time Management

Dedication and Attitude

Personality

Decision Making

Goals

Creative Questions

Customer Service

Background and Experience

Business Skills and Knowledge

Communication

Job Searching and Scheduling

Knowledge of the Company

043. How would you handle a negative coworker?

Answer:

Everyone has to deal with negative coworkers - and the single best way to do so is to remain positive. You may try to build a relationship with the coworker or relate to them in some way, but even if your efforts are met with a cold shoulder, you must retain your positive attitude. Above all, stress that you would never allow a coworker's negativity to impact your own work or productivity.

As an example:

I would remember that they are human. Most people have negatives they are facing them whether at home or at work and may not be able to handle their emotion the same as others. Additionally, they may just have a genuinely negative or bad personality. With that said, I would do my best to avoid them if possible, if they are being too negative and it is affecting my work, and do not feed in to any negativity. I would do my best to stay positive around them even when they are not positive. I would ask them if they need help with their work, or just take a moment to chat with them about their day to break up the monotony.

044. What would you do if you witnessed a coworker surfing the web, reading a book, etc, wasting company time?

Answer:

The interviewer will want to see that you realize how detrimental it is for employees to waste company time, and that it is not something you take lightly. Explain the way you would adhere to company policy, whether that includes talking to the coworker yourself, reporting the behavior straight to a supervisor, or talking to someone in HR.

As an example:

I would wait a few minutes and see if they stop on their own. Some employees may use internet to check their bank account or send a quick email; no harm done. If there are strict policies on internet usage for reasons of viruses, etc., then I would remind them they are not supposed to use it. If, however, they are just abusing the internet and surfing the web and not working for a long period of time, I believe I would not have an issue with a gentle nudge and joke, prompting them to get off. It truly depends on your relationship with your coworker as this will determine your approach. If it is someone I get along with I would have no problem with talking to them about it and finding ways to include them in the project I am working on, or perhaps offer them help in projects they are working on, reminding them to spend less time on the internet. If it is someone I do not have that sort of relationship with, I would find ways to approach them while they are using the internet and discuss work, and prompt them to get off. If it continued, I would have no problem letting management know.

045. How do you handle competition among yourself and other employees?

Answer:

Healthy competition can be a great thing, and it is best to stay focused on the positive aspects of this here. Don't bring up conflict among yourself and other coworkers, and instead focus on the motivation to keep up with the great work of others, and the ways in which coworkers may be a great support network in helping to push you to new successes.

As an example:

Healthy competition is great in the workplace under certain circumstances. If a project will be rolled out with some form of competition being encouraged, it is best to present it with guidelines and "dos and donts" of healthy competition in the workplace. I would consider using a graph to highlight progress individually as well as another to show the entire team's success together. I would also consider ways to celebrate those with higher success rates and playfully encourage those with lower success rates.

046. When is it okay to socialize with co-workers?

Answer:

This question has two extreme answers (all the time, or never), and your interviewer, in most cases, will want to see that you fall somewhere in the middle. It's important to establish solid relationships with your coworkers, but never at the expense of getting work done. Ideally, relationship-building can happen with exercises of teamwork and special projects, as well as in the break room.

As an example:

I make sure to maintain healthy working relationships with my coworkers by maintaining communication paired with boundaries. We are with our coworkers more than our families, and it is imperative that we have at least cordial working environments. It is nice to learn different personalities of your coworkers, as some may be happy to be complete introverts and focus on nothing but working and going home, while others may crave and need that human interaction in order to get through each day. I make sure to say hello to everyone I see each morning and ask them how they are doing and what their day looks like at work. I try to encourage breaks

Teamwork

away from the desk at routine times each day for chit chat or walking outside, set to a reasonable time limit. This allows for a break and banter away from the desk. Each Friday it is nice to be able to ask any plans for the weekend before leaving just to bring that outside element in to the office. Each Monday it is nice to start off with, how was your weekend questions to get it out of the way and then focus on the tasks at hand. It is also ok to tell a coworker who comes over to chit chat "I can't talk right now but can I call you for a walk when I take my break?"

047. Tell me about a time when a major change was made at your last job, and how you handled it.

Answer:

Provide a set-up for the situation including the old system, what the change was, how it was implemented, and the results of the change, and include how you felt about each step of the way. Be sure that your initial thoughts on the old system are neutral, and that your excitement level grows with each step of the new change, as an interviewer will be pleased to see your adaptability.

As an example:

I was a payroll processor and used the same system for five years. I was the one who ran payroll each week and trained two others on how to use the system. I was considered the software expert and was very comfortable with my job. Management decided to implement a new software, entirely changing the process in which I worked. At first, I was nervous and upset, as I did not know what to expect. Management asked me to assist with the set up of the new software and wanted my input, which made me feel more included and valued. Once I began using the new software, I realized it had many features the old one didn't, which ended up making my job easier and more efficient. I learned as much as I could about the new software and trained my coworkers on it.

048. When delegating tasks, how do you choose which tasks go to which team members?

Answer:

The interviewer is looking to gain insight into your thought process with this question, so be sure to offer thorough reasoning behind your choice. Explain that you delegate tasks based on each individual's personal strengths, or that you look at how many other projects each person is working on at the time, in order to create the best fit possible.

As an example:

I look at workload of each staff member and see who is actually available to have more tasks added on. I may re-arrange workloads to fit the right person in to the right task. For example, if I feel there is someone with a large workload who is best suited for making the spreadsheets I need, I may re-delegate some of their work to another staff member to free up that persons time to work on the spreadsheets. Add itionally if there are members of the team who may not be a good fit for any of the tasks required for the project, I may fit them in to a role anyway such as "project assistant" or "reviewer."

049. Tell me about a time when you had to stand up for something you believed strongly about to coworkers or a supervisor.

Answer:

While it may be difficult to explain a situation of conflict to an interviewer, this is a great opportunity to display your passions and convictions, and your dedication to your beliefs. Explain not just the situation to the interviewer, but also elaborate on why it was so important to you to stand up for the issue, and how your coworker or supervisor responded to you afterward - were they more respectful? Unreceptive? Open-minded? Apologetic?

As an example:
While working in HR, we had an employee who had clearly broken policy regarding vacation time, twice. He was given a warning then broke policy again and was time for termination. Management wanted to terminate his employment – two weeks before Christmas. While I was in agreement that he needed to be let go, I was not in agreement with the timing, especially considering the reason for the termination was not due to any malicious or violent in nature offenses. I believed the employee being terminated two weeks before Christmas for what seemed to be a lower level offense (offense nonetheless) would be detrimental to morale of the other employees and caused issues for the company and grief among the rest of the staff. I also believed that given the nature of the offenses we could afford to wait just wo more weeks. Management resisted at first, wanting to be completely reactive and "show force" however once I discussed the big picture they begrudgingly agreed to wait until one week after Christmas. Although we didn't see eye to eye always, management realized that I brought a different perspective to the table and was a valuable member of the team and began coming to me to discuss other issues as they arose when they though their decisions may affect the entire workforce.

050. Tell me about a time when you helped someone finish their work, even though it wasn't "your job."

Answer:
Though you may be frustrated when required to pick up someone else's slack, it's important that you remain positive about lending a hand. The interviewer will be looking to see if you're a team player, and by helping someone else finish a task that he or she couldn't manage alone, you show both your willingness to help the team succeed, and your own competence.

As an example:
Our department hired an intern who was having a lot of difficulties figuring out how to use the large-scale copier. They were handed a packet by another coworker and told to make 75 copies... and just told "do it." After many hours of anguish and ruined reams of paper, the intern sat down and looked defeated. I let them know they should take a break and get some fresh air. When they came back in, I took time to show them how to use the copier (since no one else did), and then went back to my work. At the end f the day I set aside time to go back over and relieve her of her duties so she could start packing up and I finished the last few packets of copies for her and helped her staple the last few sets. I walked her through every inch of the machine and how to use it, and she came back the next day refreshed and knew someone was on her side to assist with her learning experience.

051. What are the challenges of working on a team? How do you handle this?

Answer:

There are many obvious challenges to working on a team, such as handling different perspectives, navigating individual schedules, or accommodating difficult workers. It's best to focus on one challenge, such as individual team members missing deadlines or failing to keep commitments, and then offer a solution that clearly addresses the problem. For example, you could organize weekly status meetings for your team to discuss progress or assign shorter deadlines in order to keep the long-term deadline on schedule.

As an example:

Sometimes the biggest challenge is simply when everyone on the team has a different idea on how it should be completed. During these times, I make sure to hear everyone's opinions and thoughts, because that is all people really want is to feel heard. If we decide collectively that an idea someone had was not the one we were going to pursue to complete the project, then I make sure to find ways for that team member to still be included. I may ask them to take on an entire portion of the project, or come up with another idea, or perhaps improve on someone else's idea. Alternately, I may ask that team member to pick the best idea they heard and run with that one, so they still feel like they are in a bit of control and not just following along with the rest.

052. Do you value diversity in the workplace?

Answer:

Diversity is important in the workplace in order to foster an environment that is accepting, equalizing, and full of different perspectives and backgrounds. Be sure to show your awareness of these issues and stress the importance of learning from others' experiences.

As an example:

Diversity in the workplace is extremely important. Different backgrounds and personal experiences are what make a team thrive. Everyone brings something different to the table. If a team is working on a large project together, multiple people who are very similar to each other will bring very limited insight. Adding those with different viewpoints is crucial to a project, as it allows for better insight as to what others may think or feel when presented with the end product. For example, someone with the background of obtaining their masters degree and getting straight into the workforce brings with them many years of higher education and additional learning of concepts and ideas others may not be aware of. On the other hand, someone with less college education and more hands-on work experience will bring to the table practical knowledge of what actually works and does not work in the "real world", not just in a textbook. A great way to pair both types of individuals would be to have the college educated team member present ideals and strategies learned in school and allow the experienced team member to provide insight as to how to properly implement said strategy.

053. How would you handle a situation in which a coworker was not accepting of someone else's diversity?

Answer:

Explain that it is important to adhere to company policies regarding diversity, and that you would talk to the relevant supervisors or management team. When it is appropriate, it could also be best to talk to the coworker in question about the benefits of alternate perspectives - if you can handle the situation yourself, it's best not to bring resolvable issues to management.

As an example:

In my role as Sales Manager, I brought in a new salesman who was new to the country and was not as fluent in our foreign language as the rest of the staff. Most staff members were accepting of the "new guy" however we did have one seasoned staff member having a hard time with the addition. He was frustrated by the fact it was a little hard to communicate as well as did not understand what value the new person brought to the table if they could not speak our language as fluently. I explained to the employee that we value diversity and the new staff member spoke enough of our language to communicate the basics, was taking language courses on their own time in order to better communicate. I informed the seasoned team member that the new employee had a tremendous track record with high sales in his last position and brought new ideas we could implement to our process. I encouraged the seasoned employee to try to get to know the "new guy" a little more and while I understood his frustration and where he was coming from, that I also believed that given time, he would warm up to him and see his value like I did when I hired him. It is important to attempt to see both sides of a situation and try to learn where their views are coming from or why, instead of make someone feel as though they are being "forced" in to changing their beliefs or viewpoints.

054. Are you rewarded more from working on a team, or accomplishing a task on your own?

Answer:

It's best to show a balance between these two aspects - your employer wants to see that you're comfortable working on your own, and that you can complete tasks efficiently and well without assistance. However, it's also important for your employer to see that you can be a team player, and that you understand the value that multiple perspectives and efforts can bring to a project.

As an example:

While I am completely capable of and comfortable with working alone, I would have to say I do enjoy accomplishing goals more with a team. Since I am a natural leader and people person, I feel very rewarded by accomplishing a goal with a team. I enjoy motivating others along the way, helping them to see their own unique potential, learning from others, and celebrating a goal completed together.

4

Creativity

Leadership

Teamwork

Deadlines and Time Management

Dedication and Attitude

Personality

Decision Making

Goals

Creative Questions

Customer Service

Background and Experience

Business Skills and Knowledge

Communication

Job Searching and Scheduling

Knowledge of the Company

055. Tell me about a time when you didn't meet a deadline.

Answer:

Ideally, this hasn't happened - but if it has, make sure you use a minor example to illustrate the situation, emphasize how long ago it happened, and be sure that you did as much as you could to ensure that the deadline was met. Additionally, be sure to include what you learned about managing time better or prioritizing tasks in order to meet all future deadlines.

As an example:

I rarely, if ever miss a deadline. With that said, I do recall about two years ago I missed a deadline in submitting a report to the finance department. The problem ended up being that I had taken on too many projects all at once, and then had a couple of "urgent" unexpected issues thrown in as well that same week. I failed to ask for help, thinking I could do it all on my own and not wanting to give my supervisor the impression that I couldn't handle the job. What happened though was that I did let the supervisor down and when I sat down to discuss the issue with them they assured me that if I had just kept the communication open about my workload, they would have helped pick up the slack. From then on, I made sure to be more open with my supervisor with my current workload and express any concerns I have with deadlines. I have not missed a deadline since, and my relationship with my team mates and productivity within the department have both improved along with the more open communication.

056. How do you eliminate distractions while working?

Answer:

With the increase of technology and the ease of communication, new distractions arise every day. Your interviewer will want to see that you are still able to focus on work, and that your productivity has not been affected, by an example showing a routine you employ in order to stay on task.

As an example:
Each morning, I look over the days tasks and prepare for what I need to do. I check my e-mail, messages, and other personal items and then put away my personal devices. I make sure my family and friends know that I check messages only during breaks, and that if there is an emergency they have a good phone number to reach me. During breaks during the work week, I do not engage in a lot of social media, as that can drag in to the work day. On my breaks I prefer to walk, read, check in with a coworker for a few minute chat, or message a family or friend to say hello then it is back to work.

057. **Tell me about a time when you worked in a position with a weekly or monthly quota to meet. How often were you successful?**

Answer:
Your numbers will speak for themselves, and you must answer this question honestly. If you were regularly met your quotas, be sure to highlight this in a confident manner and don't be shy in pointing out your strengths in this area. If your statistics are less than stellar, try to point out trends in which they increased toward the end of your employment, and show reflection as to ways you can improve in the future.

As an example:
I consistently meet my deadlines every quarter. I take what the company gives me as a quota then I add my own personal goal to that. This way, I have something higher to work toward, and allows

wiggle room if I am able to meet just the company goal and not my own as well. I try not to focus too much on the daily sales but rather do a monthly check. This allows for me to not spend too much wasted time on worrying about progress while still making sure I am on target.

058. Tell me about a time when you met a tough deadline, and how you were able to complete it.

Answer:

Explain how you were able to prioritize tasks, or to delegate portions of an assignments to other team members, in order to deal with a tough deadline. It may be beneficial to specify why the deadline was tough - make sure it's clear that it was not a result of procrastination on your part. Finally, explain how you were able to successfully meet the deadline, and what it took to get there in the end.

As an example:

I was placed with the large task of submitting a state report I had never done before, due to my coworkers sudden absence. I researched the topic on my own downtime when I could, reached out to other companies to see how they were completing the project, and I found an online training I could take during business hours. With permission from my boss, I delegated my clerical duties to the department secretary until I was able to finish the state report. I was able to submit it ahead of schedule and it added value to my job and me as an employee, as I was asked to assist with other projects after that, received a great performance review and raise during subsequent evaluation period.

059. How do you stay organized when you have multiple projects on your plate?

Answer:
The interviewer will be looking to see that you can manage your time and work well - and being able to handle multiple projects at once, and still giving each the attention it deserves, is a great mark of a worker's competence and efficiency. Go through a typical process of goal-setting and prioritizing, and explain the steps of these to the interviewer, so he or she can see how well you manage time.

As an example:
I keep an ongoing list of tasks on a notepad and Outlook calendar. Each morning when I arrive to work, I look at my Outlook calendar and I review the written list of tasks that I had added the day before on a notepad throughout the day, and prioritize what needs to be done that day and what can wait. For the tasks that can be done later in the week, I utilize the calendar feature in Outlook to put tasks on specific dates, so a reminder pops up prompting me to complete the task. Of the items on the list that can not wait, I choose the quickest and complete those first. Then I dive in to the more complex tasks. During the day when urgent items arise that put me off my schedule, I revisit my Outlook calendar and written list and constantly adjust accordingly. I also keep in communication with my team mates and let them know if there are any items I could use assistance with if they have downtime.

060. How much time during your workday do you spend on "auto-pilot?"

Answer:

While you may wonder if the employer is looking to see how efficient you are with this question (for example, so good at your job that you don't have to think about it), but in almost every case, the employer wants to see that you're constantly thinking, analyzing, and processing what's going on in the workplace. Even if things are running smoothly, there's usually an opportunity somewhere to make things more efficient or to increase sales or productivity. Stress your dedication to ongoing development and convey that being on "auto-pilot" is not conducive to that type of success.

As an example:

I am very good at my job and do find myself going in to "auto-pilot" often. With that said, when I complete a project or task, I take time to review the completed project to assure accuracy. If I get the project done with downtime to spare after, I may try to test out a different method of completion to see if there are ways to improve the process. Sometimes there is and sometimes there simply isn't, however, I constantly find ways to utilize my time in the most effective and proficient manner.

061. How do you handle deadlines?

Answer:

The most important part of handling tough deadlines is to prioritize tasks and set goals for completion, as well as to delegate or eliminate unnecessary work. Lead the interviewer through a general scenario and display your competency through your ability to organize and set priorities, and most importantly, remain calm.

As an example:
I utilize my Outlook calendar for ongoing tasks that I know have to be completed on a recurring basis. For example, every Monday I have to submit my sales report, and every Wednesday I have to file. If there are any special projects coming up that I need to prepare for, I will set aside time and reminders on my calendar to prepare for the upcoming project. I also take time every morning when I get to work to review the tasks I have that day, and do the same at the end of each day as well to be sure I completed everything I needed to and prepare for the next day. If I feel that I am unable to meet a deadline for some reason, I communicate this with the department I am working with and see if any adjustments need to be made. Communication is key. Additionally, I am constantly mindful of the need to adjust my schedule accordingly if urgent projects arise.

062. Tell me about your personal problem-solving process.

Answer:
Your personal problem-solving process should include outlining the problem, coming up with possible ways to fix the problem, and setting a clear action plan that leads to resolution. Keep your answer brief and organized, and explain the steps in a concise, calm manner that shows you are level-headed even under stress.

As an example:
When I was working as an equipment mechanic, I began experiencing difficulty in managing the amount of work coming in from multiple project managers in my company. Each of them started pairing me as the technician over their client's equipment. I tried to tell some of them no, and I was told I was not a team player.

I ended up discussing with the shop foreman what the issue was and explained I was a team player but simply did not have enough time in the day to finish all of the jobs they were giving me. I started a scheduling board in my work area where I put what jobs I had, who the project manager was, what phase I was in with each project, and expected completion time. This allowed for all project managers to clearly see my workload, and better understand and appreciate the work I was doing, while allowing them to figure out if they wanted to pursue someone else to repair their client's equipment or wait for me to have an opening.

063. What sort of things at work can make you stressed?

Answer:

As it's best to stay away from negatives, keep this answer brief and simple. While answering that nothing at work makes you stressed will not be very believable to the interviewer, keep your answer to one generic principle such as when members of a team don't keep their commitments, and then focus on a solution you generally employ to tackle that stress, such as having weekly status meetings or intermittent deadlines along the course of a project.

As an example:

When someone I work with is not pulling their weight, it can be stressful if it ends up affecting my job negatively. During these times I remain calm and talk it out with the team. I offer assistance when I can and work on ways to better the situation. I do my best to maintain a positive and pleasant attitude, since acting out negatively will do nothing but make the situation worse. I was working on a project with three coworkers. We each had specific tasks that all tied into each other's tasks. If one of us fell behind, we all fell behind.

Deadlines and Time Management

> One co-worker was consistently behind the rest of us and the entire project was falling behind. I pulled the coworker aside and asked them if they needed assistance and explained to them that their lackof promptness was making the rest of us fall behind. I had the conversation in a very non-accusatory manner and kept things light. I offered helpful suggestions on ways they can improve their timeliness and then suggested we have daily morning meetings as a team to see where each of us was at. This allowed for more transparency amongst the team and opened a door for conversations on ways for that coworker to improve, which ended up helping us complete the project on time.

064. How do you outwardly respond to stress in the workplace? How do you calm yourself down when you are feeling stressed?

Answer:

> This is a trick question - your interviewer wants to hear that you don't look any different when you're stressed, and that you don't allow negative emotions to interfere with your productivity. As far as how you solve your stress, it's best if you have a simple solution mastered, such as simply taking deep breaths and counting to 10 to bring yourself back to the task at hand.

As an example:

> When I begin to feel stressed about a situation at work, I sometimes tend to get very quiet and take too long to think of the right response I want to give or message I want to relay to the team. In these instances, I know that it is important to let the team know that while I am feeling a little stressed at the moment, I willbe ok and am just thinking of the proper way to handle the situation. I make sure to

take a deep breath, maintain composure, smile and say I am going to take a quick break. I remove myself from the situation and step outside, or even sit for a moment in the breakroom and read a book. If staff ask me what I am doing I just simply tell them lightheartedly I needed a moment to think of how I am going to awesomely respond to the situation, or if it is a more serious topic or situation I may say I just needed a moment to recharge. Then I regroup and rejoin my team.

065. Are you good at multi-tasking? Give some examples of how you successfully multi-tastk?

Answer:

Some people can, and some people can't. The most important part of multi-tasking is to keep a clear head at all times about what needs to be done, and what priority each task falls under. Explain how you evaluate tasks to determine priority, and how you manage your time in order to ensure that all are completed efficiently.

As an example:

I am a good multi-tasker because I am able to respond to changes quickly. I keep running lists of what I am working on so if I have interruptions or urgent projects that take me away from my existing tasks, I am able to quickly go back to what I was working on.

066. How many hours per week do you work?

Answer:

Many people get tricked by this question, thinking that answering more hours is better - however, this may cause an employer to wonder why you have to work so many hours in order to get the work done that other people can do in a shorter amount of time. Give a fair estimate of hours that it should take you to complete a job and explain that you are also willing to work extra whenever needed.

As an example:
If I am working a full time forty-hour work week job, then that is what I work. Lets be honest we are human… so there have been times where I was not feeling well so I was slow, or having some off weeks where I may have only worked thirty eight hours or so, however, I did not miss any deadlines and as soon as I was feeling better I was back at my usual work speed and productivity hours. On the other hand, if I feel I need to work any overtime I will only do so if I have permission from the supervisor first. There was one instance when I had an emergency arise and it was time for me to leave, however if I left, then it would have made things worse for the company and the client, so I did stay an extra thirty minutes to complete the task, however I immediately called my supervisor of the issue and why I stayed, so they were aware.

067. How many times per day do you check your email?

Answer:

While an employer wants to see that you are plugged into modern technology, it is also important that the number of times you check your email per day is relatively low - perhaps two to three times per day (dependent on the specific field you're in). Checking email is often a great distraction in the workplace, and while it is important to remain connected, much correspondence can simply be handled together in the morning and afternoon.

As an example:
> I check my e-mail about three or four times a day. Typically, when I arrive to the office, before and after lunch, and before I leave for the day. There may be instances when things are slow in the office and I check less, or there may be times when I am waiting on an e-mail containing information I need to start a certain task, or I am in communication with a customer back and forth about an important topic, so I may check or respond more frequently. On an average day though, no more than about four times per day.

5

Creativity

Leadership

Teamwork

Deadlines and Time Management

Dedication and Attitude

Personality

Decision Making

Goals

Creative Questions

Customer Service

Background and Experience

Business Skills and Knowledge

Communication

Job Searching and Scheduling

Knowledge of the Company

068. Tell me about a time when you worked additional hours to finish a project.

Answer:

It's important for your employer to see that you are dedicated to your work, and willing to put in extra hours when required or when a job calls for it. However, be careful when explaining why you were called to work additional hours - for instance, did you have to stay late because you set goals poorly earlier in the process? Or on a more positive note, were you working additional hours because a client requested for a deadline to be moved up on short notice? Stress your competence and willingness to give 110% every time.

As an example:

I have worked additional hours to complete a project on numerous occasions. I try to only work additional hours when necessary, to avoid burnout. I also make sure that my superiors are aware of and have approved the need for additional hours. One example recently was I noticed I was part of a team working on updating the company website every morning until project completion. My role was to assign the daily schedule and tasks to each member of the team. I noticed that since we all got in at the same time, the start time of the project was always delayed. I requested to be able to arrive at work fifteen minutes early each day to log on and work on the schedule so it would be ready when the others got to work. I still needed to complete my afternoon duties which resulted in fifteen minutes of overtime each day but because my supervisor approved it, they were ok with it. The additional time allowed for the project to run more smoothly, be completed on time, and allowed for me to not fall behind on the rest of my afternoon duties as well.

Dedication and Attitude

069. Tell me about a time when your performance exceeded the duties and requirements of your job.

Answer:

If you're a great candidate for the position, this should be an easy question to answer - choose a time when you truly went above and beyond the call of duty and put in additional work or voluntarily took on new responsib-ilities. Remain humble, and express gratitude for the learning opportunity, as well as confidence in your ability to give a repeat performance.

As an example:

I was placed in charge of the annual employee benefits open enrollment. My duties were to just simply provide the necessary forms for employees to complete and collect them. I ended up preparing packets electronically as well as made hard copies available for field staff who had no access to computers to stop by and pick up. I had folders clearly labeled and check off lists ready for both distribution and collection. I made cover sheets with a list of items in the packet, what they were, why we need them, and which were mandatory, and which were not. I also made a list of each health benefit we provided and links to more information. With the increase in information provided up front, it minimized need for time taken to answer questions employees had. It offered more of a "self serve" approach. With the organized system of distribution and collection, it allowed my coworkers to be able to step in and pick up some of the duties if I was unavailable.

070. What is your driving attitude about work?

Answer:

There are many possible good answers to this question, and the interviewer primarily wants to see that you have a great passion for the job and that you will remain motivated in your career if hired. Some specific driving forces behind your success may include hard work, opportunity, growth potential, or success.

As an example:
My attitude about work is being grateful to be afforded the opportunity to serve others. I enjoy working in a company where I am passionate about the services we provide and what drives me is customer satisfaction. If I am well equipped to do my job and supported by management, I am better suited to deliver customer service.

071. Do you take work home with you?

Answer:
It is important to first clarify that you are always willing to take work home when necessary, but you want to emphasize as well that it has not been an issue for you in the past. Highlight skills such as time management, goal-setting, and multi-tasking, which can all ensure that work is completed at work.

As an example:
I believe it is good to maintain a healthy work-life balance so I do my best to be proficient in managing my time wisely during the work day so I do not have to take work home. I am however willing to step up and work late or take work home in instances where there is an emergency or to assist with a short term or occasional project that will benefit the company in the long run.

facebook.com/vibrantpublishers

072. Describe a typical work day to me.

Answer:

There are several important components in your typical work day, and an interviewer may derive meaning from any or all of them, as well as from your ability to systematically lead him or her through the day. Start at the beginning of your day and proceed chronologically, making sure to emphasize steady productivity, time for review, goal-setting, and prioritizing, as well as some additional time to account for unexpected things that may arise.

As an example:
Getting to work and getting all potential distractions out of the way is imperative. This includes checking in with coworkers and boss, checking work email, and personal messages first to make sure that there is nothing that has come up that may take you from your work. Once all coworkers have been addressed and messages have been checked, it is important to look at the days tasks that were planned and get started. If something arises that takes priority over what you are working on, it is important to be sure that you have marked where you left off so you can go back to it later that day. Checking in with coworkers and attending meetings if needed may also be a part of the schedule.

073. How would you handle not getting a promotion you interview for at your current employer?

Answer:

The employer wants to see how you would handle disappointment and if you harbour resentment easily. They also want to see how you answer this question for them during the interview and if you seem sincere in your reply. Employers want to be sure that you understand that sometimes management decisions are made for the best of the company and employees up for promotions, and that you understand everything has its own time and place. They want to see how resilient you are as well and how you would move forward.

As an example:

A few years ago, I interviewed for a promotion I was pretty sure I was going to get. I interviewed along with a coworker and three outside candidates. I did not get the job, and my coworker did. I was actually assigned to report to them as my new lead staff when the boss was away. While this was an adjustment at first, I was able to maintain professionalism, continue to work with my coworker and actually learn from them along the way. I took it as a moment to regain my thoughts and refocus my path. I did end up interviewing again for a promotion when another became available, and because of my patience, and continued learning and positive attitude, I got the promotion the second time around.

074. Are you open to receiving feedback and criticisms on your job performance, and adjusting as necessary?

Answer:

This question has a pretty clear answer - yes - but you'll need to display knowledge as to why this is important. Receiving feedback and criticism is one thing, but the most important part of that process is to then implement it into your daily work. Keep a good attitude, and express that you always appreciate constructive feedback.

As an example:

I enjoy receiving input about my performance because it helps to identify ways to improve and also provides insight as to what my supervisor is looking for and what they are paying attention to. If a supervisor is able to deliver feedback in a positive and non-demeaning manner, I am always all ears and open to suggestions for improvement. There have been a few times when a supervisor offered constructive criticism that I actually implemented in my daily job duties and helped me to drastically cut down on wasted time on certain tasks.

075. What inspires you?

Answer:

You may find inspiration in nature, reading success stories, or mastering a difficult task, but it's important that your inspiration is positively-based and that you're able to listen and tune into it when it appears. Keep this answer generally based in the professional world, but where applicable, it may stretch a bit into creative exercises in your personal life that, in turn, help you in achieving career objectives.

As an example:

I am inspired by the success of others. When I see team mates around me succeeding, that motivates me to keep going and succeed in my own role. I enjoy being in a role where I am free to motivate and encourage others. When the team is all positive and working well together and succeeding in the company mission, it makes going to work a lot easier. Alternate response could be I am inspired by books. I read frequently and often find myself able to feel relaxed and at peace when I read. Reading helps me sleep better and wake up refreshed for work. I also find myself feeling more creative at work when I read more, and at times even drawing ideas from certain books I read, and implementing those ideas in to the workplace.

076. How do you inspire others?

Answer:

This may be a difficult question, as it is often hard to discern the effects of inspiration in others. Instead of offering a specific example of a time when you inspired someone, focus on general principles such as leading by example that you employ in your professional life. If possible, relate this to a quality that someone who inspired you possessed, and discuss the way you have modified or modeled it in your own work.

As an example:

I enjoy motivating others. If someone is having a hard time with a project, or having a bad day, I find it easy to talk with them about what they are experiencing difficulties with and assure them that it will pass. I find ways to encourage them and offer suggestions on ways to keep calm during stressful times, and focus on the positives of their day, or even their life in general. I find creative ways to talk things out and remind them that no matter what, the circumstance that is bringing them down at the moment is probably not the worst thing they have ever been through and they can surely get through it. I remind them that everyone has issues and times of stress and it's ok to feel how they do, because everyone handles situations differently. I do my best to always remain positive at work even during stressful or difficult times, so I do not spread negativity.

Creativity

Leadership

Teamwork

Deadlines and Time Management

Dedication and Attitude

Personality

Decision Making

Goals

Creative Questions

Customer Service

Background and Experience

Business Skills and Knowledge

Communication

Job Searching and Scheduling

Knowledge of the Company

077. What has been your biggest success?

Answer:

Your biggest success should be something that was especially meaningful to you, and that you can talk about passionately - your interviewer will be able to see this. Always have an answer prepared for this question, and be sure to explain how you achieved success, as well as what you learned from the experience.

As an example:

Obtaining my bachelors degree took much longer than it should have due to personal circumstances that arose. I was losing motivation for a little while but I was able to keep pushing on and despite my personal obstacles, eventually graduate. I had to overcome many things to get to where I am today with my career and my education. I was happy to be able to invite my family to my graduation and see how happy it made them that I succeeded in my goal. My family helped and supported me through college and I was happy to share that with them.

078. What motivates you?

Answer:

It's best to focus on a key aspect of your work that you can target as a "driving force" behind your everyday work. Whether it's customer service, making a difference, or the chance to further your skills and gain experience, it's important that the interviewer can see the passion you hold for your career and the dedication you have to the position.

As an example:

I enjoy making a difference, not just making a paycheck. As a recruiter, I enjoy connecting people with jobs. I help people see their potential and connect them with their next big opportunity to shine. On the other hand, I help companies fill a need and find the best person for the job. I feel that at the end of the day I am making a difference and helping people, which really motivates me in my career, and makes going to work a lot easier every day.

079. What do you do when you lose motivation?

Answer:

The best candidates will answer that they rarely lose motivation, because they already employ strategies to keep themselves inspired, and because they remain dedicated to their objectives. Additionally, you may impress the interviewer by explaining that you are motivated by achieving goals and advancing, so small successes are always a great way to regain momentum.

As an example:

It is rare that I totally lose all motivation however during times where I have a heavy workload or am feeling a bit run down, I may tend to get a little tired, as anyone. During these times, in order to avoid burnout and regain motivation, I make lists of what I need to do that week and also lists of major accomplishments over the past few weeks. I will make sure to take breaks and do things to get energized, such as listening to music or taking walks. I will read up on new trends on the field I am in, perhaps coach a recent who is hoping to get their foot in the door to the field I am in or read some stories of inspiration. Often times I feel most motivated when I am energized and motivating others.

080. What do you like to do in your free time?

Answer:

What you do answer here is not nearly as important as what you don't answer - your interviewer does not want to hear that you like to drink, party, or revel in the nightlife. Instead, choose a few activities to focus on that are greater signs of stability and maturity, and that will not detract from your ability to show up to work and be productive, such as reading, cooking, or photography. This is also a great opportunity to show your interviewer that you are a well-rounded, interesting, and dynamic personality that they would be happy to hire.

As an example:

In my free time I enjoy reading, going to the movies, and bike riding. I also volunteer with the local animal shelter twice a year for their semi-annual fundraiser where I help set up the venue, check in guests, and sell raffle tickets. I also enjoy watching free webinars and attending online seminars to brush up on my field of engineering when I can.

081. What sets you apart from other workers?

Answer:

This question is a great opportunity to highlight the specific skill sets and passion you bring to the company that no one else can. If you can't outline exactly what sets you apart from other workers, how will the interviewer see it? Be prepared with a thorough outline of what you will bring to the table, in order to help the companyachieve their goals.

Personality

As an example:

I am great at project management and public speaking, which sometimes may go hand in hand. I enjoy learning everything about a project I am assigned to, and I am able to see the big picture and identify what needs to be done for each task and what staff what be a good fit for each task. Additionally, public speaking is a great trait to have when you are assigned as project manager or lead person and must lead multiple staff members and communicate with multipledepartments. I am able to present well and communicate clearly and effectively.

082. Why do you feel you are the best candidate for this position?

Answer:

Have a brief response prepared in advance for this question, as this is another very common theme in interviews (variations of the question include: "Why should I hire you, above Candidate B?" and "What can you bring to our company that Candidate B cannot?"). Make sure that your statement does not sound rehearsed and highlight your most unique qualities that show the interviewer why he or she must hire you above all the other candidates. Include specific details about your experience and special projects or recognition you've received that set you apart, and show your greatest passion, commitment, and enthusiasm for the position.

As an example:

Not only have I been in sales for over five years, but I have also been placed in leadership roles unexpectedly and suddenly, with little training, and was able to thrive. I am a fast learner and dedicated to providing the best customer service possible. It is my personal goal to not only help the company I work for, but to surpass my own sales goals each quarter while still maintaining integrity and quality of service. I want to be the best at my craft and the best version of myself that I can be. When I find a company that values their employees and provides a good product, I am motivated to work diligently to make the company look good and help them succeed. When the company succeeds, I do as well.

083. What does it take to be successful?

Answer:

Hard work, passion, motivation, and a dedication to learning - these are all potential answers to the ambiguous concept of success. It doesn't matter so much which of these values you choose as the primary means to success, or if you choose a combination of them. It is, however, absolutely key that whichever value you choose, you must clearly display in your attitude, experience, and goals.

As an example:

Never giving up is important in any success story. Some people achieve success early in their careers in terms of accomplishing their goals, and for others it may take longer. The true measure of success is just never giving up and continuing to move toward your goals. Along the way you learn from both your failures and successes, and eventually will get to where you want to be. I had a goal of getting my masters degree by the time I was thirty. I had unexpected obstacles I had to overcome and ended up not obtaining it until a few years later. I did not give up and still felt a great sense of pride and accomplishment when I did receive it, and it made it that much more special of an occasion.

084. What would be the biggest challenge in this position for you?

Answer:

Keep this answer positive and remain focused on the opportunities for growth and learning that the position can provide. Be sure that no matter what the challenge is, it's obvious that you're ready and enthusiastic to tackle it, and that you have a full awareness of what it will take to get the job done.

As an example:

The biggest challenge of this position would be that I have years of experience in engineering but for a public sector. Moving in to private sector would be an adjustment as there would be different rules and protocols to learn. With that said, I have a solid foundation and knowledge in the field and would be able to fully adjust and settle in to a new position in private sector.

085. Would you describe yourself as an introvert or an extrovert?

Answer:

There are beneficial qualities to each of these, and your answer may depend on what type of work you're involved in. However, a successful leader may be an introvert or extrovert, and similarly, solid team members may also be either. The important aspect of this question is to have the level of self-awareness required to accurately describe yourself.

As an example:

I think of myself as more of an introvert and even got into the construction field because I would be able to work alone more often or within smaller groups, and work with my hands. Over the years though I have found that part of working in construction is about team work and a lot of communication for safety reasons. I have effectively been able to overcome being a bit of an introvert and be able to effectively work as a team and have made solid bonds with the people I work with. We all know we need to work together to maintain safety out in the field, in order to go home to our families at the end of the day.

086. What are some positive character traits that you don't possess?

Answer:

If an interviewer asks you a tough question about your weaknesses, or lack of positive traits, it's best to keep your answer light-hearted and simple - for instance, express your great confidence in your own abilities, followed by a (rather humble) admittance that you could occasionally do to be humbler.

As an example:

I have a lot of positive character traits such as I am good at taking direction, a good listener, and great at problem solving. I do believe that I could work on my ability to speak up more often when I feel I need to. I have felt that I should just go with the flow and not speak up however there are times where speaking up is a necessity. Trust and communication with my supervisors would be very helpful in working toward improving this trait.

087. What is the greatest lesson you've ever learned?

Answer:
While this is a very broad question, the interviewer will be more interested in hearing what kind of emphasis you place on this value. Your greatest lesson may tie in with something a mentor, parent, or professor once told you, or you may have gleaned it from a book written by a leading expert in your field. Regardless of what the lesson is, it is most important that you can offer an example of how you've incorporated it into your life.

As an example:
I learned to not be too prideful, so prideful to ask for help when I need it. I had a boss who would continuously ask me if I needed help or check on me, which made me feel as though he thought I was not good enough or couldn't handle my job. This only made me want to push further back and not ask for help. When I ended up being very behind and burnt-out on my job, totally affecting my work performance, my boss called me aside and had a meeting with me. It was my first job in the field I went to school for and this was my first major meeting like this. He ended up telling me that he had been concerned about my workload because he saw all of the work I was taking on and that I should have asked for help when I needed it. I agreed that perhaps I should have conceded to the fact I needed help and explained that I wanted to take it all on to prove something. I learned that I should always be open with my superiors and communicate needs so that I would never be in that position again.

088. Have you ever been in a situation where one of your strengths became a weakness in an alternate setting?

Answer:

It's important to show an awareness of yourself by having an answer for this question, but you want to make sure that the weakness is relatively minor, and that it would still remain a strength in most settings. For instance, you may be an avid reader who reads anything and everything you can find but reading billboards while driving to work may be a dangerous idea.

As an example:

I have always been good at problem solving and don't mind people knowing when I am right. I was in a meeting with some new interns one afternoon at work when the manager presented a scenario to them and I blurted out the right answer. She presented another scenario and open-ended questions to which I had another response immediately. I was the only one talking and wondering why I was the only one answering these obviously easy questions. I found out later that the manager was wanting to open up dialogue with the new interns and allow for some training and learning opportunities... and I was unaware. I should have picked up on that and stayed a bit quieter. The next meeting we had, I obliged and let the interns provide the answers.

089. Who has been the most influential person in your life?

Answer:

Give a specific example (and name) to the person who has influenced your life greatly and offer a relevant anecdote about a meaningful exchange the two of you shared. It's great if their influence relates to your professional life, but this particular question opens up the possibility to discuss inspiration in your personal life as well. The interviewer wants to see that you're able to make strong connections with other individuals, and to work under the guiding influence of another person.

As an example:

My uncle has always been an inspiration to me both because of his personal and professional life. He had a career goal to become a police officer. He worked his way through college and the police academy, and despite people telling him he would not be able to make it as a policeman, he kept going anyway. Years into his career he would tell me stories of things he would see at work that he did not agree with and he always made the right decision and never let anyone else warp his opinion of what was right. He truly wanted to help make a difference and protect the community while treating everyone respectfully, and he did, no matter what anyone said. His work ethic as well as his good moral compass has always impressed me.

090. Do you consider yourself to be a "detailed" or "big picture" type of person?

Answer:

Both of these are great qualities, and it's best if you can incorporate each into your answer. Choose one as your primary type and relate it to experience or specific items from your resume. Then, explain how the other type fits into your work as well.

As an example:

I feel I have a good sense of both. These are both directly related to each other in the way that the details all tie in to the big picture, and you must understand the big picture (or end goal) in order to complete the detail or task you are assigned. On the other hand, understanding the big picture means understanding each detail that must go in to it in order to achieve the end goal. I am good at managing teams because I am able to see both.

091. What is your greatest fear?

Answer:

Disclosing your greatest fear openly and without embarrassment is a great way to show your confidence to an employer. Choose a fear that you are clearly doing work to combat, such as a fear of failure that will seem impossible to the interviewer for someone such as yourself, with such clear goals and actions plans outlined. As tempting as it may be to stick with an easy answer such as spiders, stay away from these, as they don't really tell the interviewer anything about yourself that's relevant.

As an example:

Failing to convey the message I want to get across or being misunderstood has always been a fear of mine. I have strong opinions and expertise on certain topics and I sometimes fear that when I am impassioned about a topic I may get caught up in the details and even though I may understand the big picture, the audience may be stuck on the small details and not understand the point I am trying to make.

092. What sort of challenges do you enjoy?

Answer:

The challenges you enjoy should demonstrate some sort of initiative or growth potential on your part and should also be

Personality

in line with your career objectives. Employers will evaluate consistency here, as they analyze critically how the challenges you look forward to are related to your ultimate goals.

As an example:
I have come across many challenges in keeping up with changing technology over the years. As an Accountant for the last twenty years, I have had to learn many different computerized software programs in my field. I have had to learn to adjust and adapt to many different ways companies conduct business, and many different software platforms along the way. Technology is always changing and seems at times challenging to keep up with. It seems like every time I learn a new accounting software, another comes out. I enjoy learning new programs and testing them out to see if they would be beneficial to my business or not. Finding new software goldmines that actually help boost business or make my job easier is always a great reward to the challenge of learning a new software.

093. Tell me about a time you were embarrassed. How did you handle it?

Answer:
No one wants to bring up times they were embarrassed in a job interview, and it's probably best to avoid an anecdote here. However, don't shy away from offering a brief synopsis, followed by a display of your ability to laugh it off. Show the interviewer that it was not an event that impacted you significantly.

As an example:
There was a time I was late for a meeting. When I arrived, the other attendees were clearly irritated with me as I tried my best to slink in un-noticed. I had messaged my boss to let her know I was ten

minutes late but did not give a reason. When I was put on the spot in front of everyone, I went ahead and showed them that one of the heels had broken off of one of my shoes and I was now walking with a lop-sided limp. The other attendees mostly chuckled, and as embarrassed as I was, I laughed it off as well, apologized and told them that I had tried to fix it but because I didn't want to keep them waiting any longer, decided to limp into the meeting anyway. We had a good laugh and went on with the meeting.

094. What is your greatest weakness?

Answer:

This is another one of the most popular questions asked in job interviews, so you should be prepared with an answer already. Try to come up with a weakness that you have that can actually be a strength in an alternate setting - such as, "I'm very detail-oriented and like to ensure that things are done correctly, so I sometimes have difficulty in delegating tasks to others." However, don't try to mask obvious weaknesses - if you have little practical experience in the field, mention that you're looking forward to great opportunities to further your knowledge.

As an example:

I have had a problem with how to answer this question for many years. When I was younger, I really did not know how to answer this question and did not have anything to say. I have learned over the years that the best answer for this for myself seems to be that I do like to make others happy and have a hard time saying no, so much so that I have put others over myself when I shouldn't have, and it affected me negatively, and in turn affected my work performance. With time and experience and self awareness, I have learned that while I am still able to be myself and naturally help others, I also now have to put healthy boundaries in place so I am still able to help others but not to the point where I am taking away from my own performance.

095. What are the three best adjectives to describe you in a work setting?

Answer:
While these three adjectives probably already appear somewhere on your resume, don't be afraid to use them again in order to highlight your best qualities. This is a chance for you to sell yourself to the interviewer, and to point out traits you possess that other candidates do not. Use the most specific and accurate words you can think of and elaborate shortly on how you embody each.

As an example:
I am dedicated to performing my job the best of my abilities. I am passionate about the field I am in. I am organized and able to manage multiple changing priorities without losing track of where I am at with my work load and schedule.

096. What are the three best adjectives to describe you in your personal life?

Answer:
Ideally, the three adjectives that describe you in your personal life should be similar to the adjectives that describe you in your professional life. Employers appreciate consistency, and while they may be understanding of you having an alternate personality outside of the office, it's best if you employ similar

principles in your actions both on and off the clock.

As an example:

I am loyal to my friends and family and always there when they need to talk or work through problems. I am caring and genuinely want my family and friends to be happy and successful and am always motivating them and cheering them on. I am extremely clean and tidy and like to keep my house clean and organized.

097. What type of worker are you?

Answer:

This is an opportunity for you to highlight some of your greatest assets. Characterize some of your talents such as dedicated, self-motivated, detail-oriented, passionate, hard-working, analytical, or customer service focused. Stay away from your weaker qualities here and remain on the target of all the wonderful things that you can bring to the company.

As an example:

I am very hard working and dedicated worker. I always get the job done and will even offer assistance to my coworkers if I am finished and they are struggling. I recently was put in charge of creating a new filing system and went above and beyond by typing out an index for each team member to keep at their desk to easily locate files they were looking for. I worked diligently on updating the filing system and even did some quality assurance when I transferred the files over. When I was finished I double checked my work to make sure that it was accurate and I was putting my best foot forward and doing the best I could do. Afterward, I helped my coworker finish putting together meeting agenda packets she was behind on. I am consistently dedicated to helping my team and company succeed and work hard to make sure that everything gets accomplished. If I have

Personality

downtime, I do not surf the internet or waste time; I find something else productive to do.

098. Tell me about your happiest day at work.

Answer:
Your happiest day at work should include one of your greatest professional successes, and how it made you feel. Stay focused on what you accomplished and be sure to elaborate on how rewarding or satisfying the achievement was for you.

As an example:
I was presented with a certificate of appreciation from the entire staff for working on the employee events committee. This made me very happy because it was unexpected and proved to me that the employees genuinely appreciated the hard work I had put in the events. I had many long days of planning and days where I wondered if people would even enjoy the events I put on, so when they presented me with a simple piece of paper saying they appreciated it, that meant the world to me. I was recognized for my contributions and it motivated me to keep going.

099. Tell me about your worst day at work.

Answer:
It may have been the worst day ever because of all the mistakes you made, or because you'd just had a huge argument with your best friend, but make sure to keep this answer professionally focused. Try to use an example in which something uncontrollable happened in the workplace (such as an important member of a team quit unexpectedly, which ruined your team's meeting with a client), and focus on the

frustration of not being in control of the situation. Keep this answer brief and be sure to end with a reflection on what you learned from the day.

As an example:

I had a big project pending and almost had all approvals needed. The only thing holding me back was I still needed the CEOs signature. Once I obtained that, I could move forward on this massive project I had worked months to secure. I went to work in a good mood, excited that after all my hard work and waiting, I would get the signature I needed and get this project moving and I found out the CEO was not going to approve the project. This hit me hard because it was so unexpected and unplanned. She wanted additional meetings and required further information before she would sign off. It took another month for full approval. What I learned from this was what questions the CEO would likely ask next time, and had the answers ready and included in the signature packet ahead of time. I also started to send a friendly reminder of the upcoming signature request a week ahead, so the CEO could review the project and prepare questions in advance and move things along more quickly.

100. What are you passionate about?

Answer:

Keep this answer professionally-focused where possible, but it may also be appropriate to discuss personal issues you are passionate about as well (such as the environment or volunteering at a soup kitchen). Stick to issues that are non-controversial and allow your passion to shine through as you explain what inspires you about the topic and how you stay actively engaged in it. Additionally, if you choose a personal passion, make sure it is one that does not detract from your

Personality

availability to work or to be productive.

As an example:
> I am passionate about helping people. This translates to all areas of my life. I enjoy helping people whether at home or at work. In the field I am in which is nursing, I get to help people every day. I find myself helping people in unexpected ways as well, such as just lending an ear to listen when others have a bad day, or doing little kind gestures to strangers when I am out in public like opening a door, giving a smile, putting away a shopping cart. In my free time I volunteer with the local homeless shelter and help set up their evening meals and offer case management referrals. Keeping productive and helping people motivates me to keep going.

101. What is the piece of criticism you receive most often?

Answer:

An honest, candid answer to this question can greatly impress an interviewer (when, of course, it is coupled with an explanation of what you're doing to improve), but make sure the criticism is something minimal or unrelated to your career.

As an example:
> I have been told I need to slow down a little when I get focused on a project. I tend to get involved and want to finish the project and see it through to completion so badly, that I have made a couple of mistakes along the way that needed to be corrected later. While the mistakes were not big or costly, they still could have been avoided by taking more time. I have learned to pace myself more and learned the value of taking time to assure the project is done with both quality and promptness. I stop to check my work occasionally as well, which helps me to keep it moving at a pace I feel is quick while still being able to maintain quality and fix mistakes as I go instead of complete

it fast and wait until the very end to double check for errors.

102. What type of work environment do you succeed the most in?

Answer:

Be sure to research the company and the specific position before heading into the interview. Tailor your response to fit the job you'd be working in and explain why you enjoy that type of environment over others. However, it's also extremely important to be adaptable, so remain flexible to other environments as well.

As an example:

I find myself most successful in an environment where the management has an open-door policy. When I am able to communicate with my superiors frequently and without feeling like a bother, I am more likely to be open to discuss my workload, my ideas, and also take constructive criticism. Open communication along the way during any project makes it much easier for me to complete my work.

103. Are you an emotional person?

Answer:

It's best to focus on your positive emotions - passion, happiness, motivations - and to stay away from other extreme emotions that may cause you to appear unbalanced. While you want to display your excitement for the job, be sure to remain level-headed and cool at all times, so that the interviewer knows you're not the type of person who lets emotions take you over and get in the way of your work.

As an example:

I have feelings of course, and I am able to control emotion and maintain professionalism in the workplace. I find that people who tend to let their emotion take over while they are at work are a distraction to others as well as they negatively affect their own work performance. I am passionate about my job and what I do, and motivated in my career. Because I am so passionate, I may be very excited about an accomplishment, or very negatively affected by not meeting a deadline, or other not so good happening at work. I like to think about it, talk it out if I need to, and immediately make a plan of action for what my next move will be. Staying positive and levelheaded at work is important for yourself, your coworkers, and your company.

This page is intentionally left blank

7

Creativity

Leadership

Teamwork

Deadlines and Time Management

Dedication and Attitude

Personality

Decision Making

Goals

Creative Questions

Customer Service

Background and Experience

Business Skills and Knowledge

Communication

Job Searching and Scheduling

Knowledge of the Company

104. Have you come across any decision-making situations in the past?

Answer:

The interviewer is offering you a chance to share your experiences and it is your turn to grab this opportunity and impress them. You must answer answer in a way where you are prioritizing the fact that decision-making is the most essential part in managing any organization. Highlight situations and incidents where you had to make important decisions and be sure to convey that you were careful in your thought process and consulted with higher officials when necessary. Walk the interviewer through your experiences so they may get a glimpse into your decision-making process.

As an example:

I have continuously had jobs where I was in charge of making decisions at work. I have had to make split second decisions in the field as a construction worker many times. There are some days that just don't go as planned and you have to make adjustments, and that means deciding which way to go in order to get the job done. Recently I was on a site repaving a parking lot, and a coworker had to leave early. Without him, certain parts of the job would be put on hold until he returned the next day. I had to decide whether or not to keep moving and work around those parts we needed him for and go back and re-work what we missed when he returned, or stop that portion of the job for the day and work on repainting strips on a completed portion. We ended up beginning on repainting the stripes on an already finished and dried portion of the lot and picked up on the rest the next day. This ended up being a better use of time.

105. How will you make decisions under pressure?

Answer:

The first step you should do is prioritizing issues. This will help you to take up the most important problem first. Communicate in a calm and confident manner and use cues from your experience to find solutions. If the problem is complex, don't just depend on your intuition but also consult those who are closest to the ground in managing the problem.

As an example:
I am constantly analyzing my priorities. There are times where tasks may change throughout the week or even day, where added work comes in, changing deadlines, and added pressure. What I do is evaluate what needs to be done first and what can wait and tackle each task one at a time. If a project or task arises that takes precedence over the rest and I know that it will mean the rest of my workload will get behind, I communicate the issue with my superiors or with the others involved with the project on my team.

106. Do you think it is always important to make ethically correct decisions?

Answer:

The interviewer wants to know you understand that opportunistic decisions are short lived. Ethics should be the foundation of every business and the absence of it could even lead to costly legal concerns. Show the interviewer you know how important responsible decision making is to any organization.

As an example:

It is very important to be ethical in all decision-making processes. Cutting corners to save time or money is not a good thing if it means that there were things done illegally, immorally, or that compromise the integrity of the employees or customers of the company. Decision making should be always based around a strong ethical foundation whether it be around office processes, company budget management, or employee management.

107. Does your emotional maturity play a role in making decisions?

Answer:

A leader's emotional maturity does play a role while making decisions. You should always keep your decisions simple, balanced and rational and never let emotions come in the way. You must be resistant from being swayed away by any desired outcome.

As an example:

Emotional maturity is always a driving factor in a leader's ability to successfully lead. For example, recently I was put in the position where I was the new manager over a staff that included a colleague I had worked with many years prior at a previous employer, and we did not always see eye to eye when we worked together. Much time had gone by and at this point when I came on board, the individual was up for a promotion and I was on the interview panel. I was able to set aside our rocky history and see him for the professional he had become, and after the interview I knew he was the best person for the job. I did give him the promotion and continued to work on our professional working relationship for the good of our current company.

108. Do you think decision making should be done by the manager or by a team?

Answer

Decision-making can be done either by the manager or by a team; it entirely depends upon the type of problem. The manager must allow the group members to share their views if the problem needs to be handled with expert assistance. Ultimately the final decision must be taken by the manager himself after considering all the possibilities.

As an example:

A good manager knows how to have the final say in a decision-making process after he or she has taken into account all possible outcomes and differing points of view and input from the entire team. Of course there may be instances where a manager needs to make a sudden or split second decision, or it may not make sense to consult with the team first, however in most instances a manager should at least get input and decide what is best for the team and the company.

109. Good business decisions are based on sound empirical evidence. Do you agree with this view?

Answer:

Intuitions are useful during threatening situations, but rational decisions become even more reliable when made on strong empirical evidence. Hence, this view is indeed right.

As an example:

While forward thinking is key for progression, it is useful when making business decisions to always consider historical facts and what you already know. Without this, you risk repeating mistakes or neglecting to address certain things you should have. Recently at the marketing company I work for, we sent a survey out to our clients. We neglected to review the results and reporting from the last survey we had conducted and if we had done so, we would have known that it was probably better to send the survey out right before the weekend and allow it to be open for three days, instead of send it mid week and only have it open for a day.Had we revisited historical facts we would have gotten more responses and a better outcome.

110. When do you think a team can be involved in decision-making?

Answer:

A problem which arises at the team level must be discussed by all the team members in order to identify a suitable solution for the problem. The manager's experiences can be called for if necessary.

As an example:

When the topic of the decision is something that is totally outside of the realm of expertise and experience of any team member and would only confuse the individuals on the team, careful consideration needs to made as to how to approach the team for input. Misunderstandings may cause confusion. It's important to include the team if you have all information gathered and presented in a clear manner so an informed decision may be made. It is good to get input from team members for the best outcome so everyone feels they have a say. Ultimately the manager needs to oversee the process and be the final decision maker.

111. Do you think decision-making is a form of planning? If yes, what is the similarity between the two?

Answer:

Yes, decision-making is no doubt a form of planning. As in planning, decision-making also affects a future course of action and involves choosing from alternatives. Planning, along with its procedures, policies and objectives, is an outcome of decision-making.

As an example:

There is no planning without decision making. The need for sound decisions before any solid plan is important so the project runs smoothly.

112. In a financial services company like ours how do you think decisions should be made?

Answer:

The decisions should be arrived after deep analysis of the hard data and not merely based on your personal instincts, which may lead to disaster.

As an example:

An in-depth review of all available data is important in making decisions in a financial services company. Failing to analyze data on hand may result in financial losses.

113. What are the steps to be followed in attaining a decision?

Answer:

The steps to be followed in order to arrive at a decision include problem recognition, problem analysis, finding various alternatives to solve the problem, selecting the best alternative and finally applying and verifying it for the best result possible.

As an example:

As a fast food chain manager I noticed the sales were declining at my store. I looked back over the sales records for the last few months, the staffing records, and the menu items. I noticed that we had one less employee staffed for each shift and had also removed a couple of menu items. I realized the staff shortage was causing longer wait times and customers were leaving to go to the restaurant next door, as well as we had significantly less customers in the morning rush hour due to the removal of the breakfast items. I added another staff on shift and added the breakfast items back. We were down sales for another couple of months but back on top after four months. We ended up significantly increasing sales over the next year consistently.

114. How do you make decisions?

Answer:

This is a great opportunity for you to wow your interviewer with your decisiveness, confidence, and organizational skills. Make sure that you outline a process for decision-making, and that you stress the importance of weighing your options, as well as in trusting intuition. If you answer this question skillfully and with ease, your interviewer will trust in your capability as a worker.

As an example:

I try to think about all possible outcomes and look at the big picture. Then I break down the details and decide what is most important to get done first and what can wait. Then I estimate how long it will take to complete. I communicate with my manager any issues I foresee and work out any kinks ahead of time.

115. What are the most difficult decisions for you to make?

Answer:

Explain your relationship to decision-making, and a general synopsis of the process you take in making choices. If there is a particular type of decision that you often struggle with, such as those that involve other people, make sure to explain why that type of decision is tough for you, and how you are currently engaged in improving your skills.

As an example:

Sometimes it may be difficult to make decisions that affect others in my department. For example, recently as a lead worker I had to approve and deny multiple overlapping time off requests. I knew that each person wanted certain days off and while not feasible for everyone to get the same day off, I did my best to make things as fair as possible. I spoke with individuals who had put in for the same days off and made decisions based off of who had turned in the request first or what was most urgent. I had encouraged the employees to speak openly with each other as well to determine needs and work as a team and a couple of times they came to me with solutions before I had to make a decision, which improved morale and comradery in he long run.

116. When making a tough decision, how do you gather information?

Answer:

If you're making a tough choice, it's best to gather information from as many sources as possible. Lead the interviewer through your process of taking information from people in different areas, starting first with advice from experts in your field, feedback from coworkers or other clients, and by looking analytically at your own past experiences.

As an example:

I gather information from all areas. I learn from past experiences of my own and oftentimes pull from historical data. I also consult with superiors and team mates in my field and see what works for them or if they have any insight that may help with my task.

117. Tell me about a decision you made that did not turn out well.

Answer:

Honesty and transparency are great values that your interviewer will appreciate - outline the choice you made, why you made it, the results of your poor decision - and finally (and most importantly!) what you learned from the decision. Give the interviewer reason to trust that you wouldn't make a decision like that again in the future.

As an example:

I thought it would be a good idea to start a committee to help make decisions on employee recognition events. While this was a good idea, I went about it the wrong way. I opened it up to anyone to wanted to join and did not have a solid plan in place for how we would take suggestions and implement new ideas into action. We were a little overwhelmed and unorganized and some time wasting occurred. I ended up putting the meetings on pause until I came up with a streamlined agenda we would follow, a system for taking suggestions and a plan for how we would vote on what ideas to implement. This helped to maximize time and efforts and things went more smoothly from then on.

118. Are you able to make decisions quickly?

Answer:

You may be able to make decisions quickly but be sure to communicate your skill in making sound, thorough decisions as well. Discuss the importance of making a decision quickly, and how you do so, as well as the necessity for each decision to first be well-informed.

As an example:

I tend to make decisions rather quickly. Early in my career I would make decisions quickly based off of instinct and learned that I need to be sure to trust my instinct and experience to make prompt decisions while still taking a moment to think of all possible outcomes and situations that may arise, and look at other possibilities as well. I am now able to take my initial instinct decision, think about if it is indeed the best decision and move forward from there.

This page is intentionally left blank

8

Creativity

Leadership

Teamwork

Deadlines and Time Management

Dedication and Attitude

Personality

Decision Making

Goals

Creative Questions

Customer Service

Background and Experience

Business Skills and Knowledge

Communication

Job Searching and Scheduling

Knowledge of the Company

119. Ten years ago, what were your career goals?

Answer:

In reflecting back to what your career goals were ten years ago, it's important to show the ways in which you've made progress in that time. Draw distinct links between specific objectives that you've achieved and speak candidly about how it felt to reach those goals. Remain positive, upbeat, and growth-oriented, even if you haven't yet achieved all of the goals you set out to reach.

As an example:

I was wanting to climb to the top of the ladder as quickly as possible and achieve what I thought was the height of the field I was in which was to be a Finance Director. Over the years I began working so much in Accounting that I realized once I worked in Finance Director capacities I would be detached from the day to day aspects of accounting and payroll which I truly enjoyed. In working with the Finance Director on projects I was able to see the types of things she worked on and I did not think I would enjoy that position. I reached the level of Accounting Supervisor and was able to make very good money, oversee an accounting team, and still be able to be a part of the field I loved. This was a great achievement to be happy in a career that was stable with great pay and benefits. I have learned that things take time and cannot be obtained overnight, and with time comes more wisdom and insight into what you are truly meant to do in your career.

120. Tell me about a weakness you used to have, and how you changed it.

Answer:

Choose a non-professional weakness that you used to have and outline the process you went through in order to grow past it. Explain the weakness itself, why it was problematic, the action steps you planned, how you achieved them, and the end result.

As an example:

Many years ago, I would find myself constantly in charge of conversations. This was not something necessarily bad or that I did on purpose it was just something that came naturally because I had natural leadership and outgoing qualities. I began to notice that others had a lot to say and may not want to speak up so I started to allow others more time to speak and take control of conversations. This helped me learn many things I didn't know before and translated into my work life as well. I was able to gather more input from my coworkers and be more open to new ideas and processes. I learned that I also enjoyed seeing other people open up and help them to find their voice as well.

121. Tell me about your goal-setting process.

Answer:

When describing your goal setting process, clearly outline the way that you create a goal for yourself. It may be helpful to offer an example of a particular goal you've set in the past and use this as a starting point to guide the way you created action steps, check-in points, and how the goal was eventually achieved.

As an example:

> When setting a goal, I gather as much information as possible before I begin. A few years ago, I decided to obtain my accounting certification. I checked on the basics like how much it would cost, the various outlets that offered the certification and what types, what positions required or asked for the certification, and what the cost was. I obtained study material and began studying while I registered for the test. I waited to register until I knew I was going to be able to afford to take the test and take time off to go to the testing center. I picked a testing date and set it on my calendar as a countdown and this forced myself to work hard to get as much studying as possible done and have a "no turning back" attitude. I looked at it like something that had to be done. I learned that setting deadlines for myself helps to keep me in line. I passed on the first try and obtained my certification!

122. Tell me about a time when you solved a problem by creating actionable steps to follow.

Answer:

This question will help the interviewer to see how talented you are in outlining, problem resolution, and goal setting. Explain thoroughly the procedure of outlining the problem, establishing steps to take, and then how you followed the steps (such as through check-in points along the way, or intermediary goals).

As an example:

> As the shop manager for a car mechanic I was given the task of giving a custom paint job to a classic carn that was going to be in an upcoming car show. The paint job was a large one with very intricate details and shades of paint. I first determined what was going to take

the most time to do (which would be the design), so I started on the design before the car was even dropped off. Once the car was there I took the bumpers off and painted them and set them aside, leaving the rest of the car exposed and ready to be painted. I communicated with the car owner every other day to give progress reports, and had an assistant come in to help mix the paint while I was applying to the rest of the car. I planned out which parts to paint first so they would be dry and ready for the pinstripe design, and was able to complete the project with enough time left over for the owner to give input and make changes if necessary before the car show.

123. Where do you see yourself five years from now?

Answer:

Have some idea of where you would like to have advanced to in the position you're applying for, over the next several years. Make sure that your future plans line up with you still working for the company and stay positive about potential advancement. Focus on future opportunities, and what you're looking forward to - but make sure your reasons for advancement are admirable, such as greater experience and the chance to learn, rather than simply being out for a higher salary.

As an example:

I hope to have learned more in my field and promoted to at least the next highest position. I currently am an entry level mechanic but would like to see myself maybe even as a shop foreman so I can share my knowledge and passion for building and design. I consider myself a people person and like to lift others up so getting to foreman level would help me to be able to motivate others and help them in their careers as well.

124. When in a position, do you look for opportunities to promote?

Answer:

There's a fine balance in this question - you want to show the interviewer that you have initiative and motivation to advance in your career, but not at the expense of appearing opportunistic or selfishly-motivated. Explain that you are always open to growth opportunities, and very willing to take on new responsibilities as your career advances.

As an example:

I look for opportunities to promote but only if it is a position I believe I would be a good fit for. I recently had the opportunity to interview for a higher level position with more pay and after reviewing the job description more and talking with the current incumbent I realized that I would not enjoy the position at all and did not have experience in some of the job duties either. I knew I would not be the best fit for the position and others would love the opportunity and be better at it so I passed it up. I would be willing to promote to a higher-level position still, in the specific areas I am confident in and know I could excel in so I would be able to help myself and the company grow.

125. On a scale of 1 to 10, how successful has your life been?

Answer:

Though you may still have a long list of goals to achieve, it's important to keep this answer positively-focused. Choose a high number between 7 and 9 and explain that you feel your life has been largely successful and satisfactory as a result of several specific achievements or experiences. Don't go as high as a 10, as the interviewer may not believe your response or in your ability to reason critically.

As an example:

I believe it to be about a 9. The reason being is I am satisfied with how far I have come and obstacles I have overcome to get where I am at today. I have a solid family life, am working toward obtaining the career in the field I want to be in, a steady vision on where I want to be, a roof over my head, and am generally a happy person. The reason for not giving a 10 would be because there is always room for growth, improvements, and new goals to be achieved.

126. What is your greatest goal in life?

Answer:

It's okay for this answer to stray a bit into your personal life, but best if you can keep it professionally-focused. While specific goals are great, if your personal goal doesn't match up exactly with one of the company's objectives, you're better off keeping your goal a little more generic and encompassing, such as "success in my career" or "leading a happy and fulfilling life." Keep your answer brief, and show a decisive nature - most importantly, make it clear that you've already thought about this question and know what you want.

As an example:

Living a happy and fulfilling life is my ultimate goal. Being a good person, putting my best foot forward, and looking at the positives is always something I set out to do. This pours into my work life in a positive way because the more positive I am, the easier any work day is, and the more I focus on being happy and doing a job that makes me happy, the harder I work because I believe in the company I work at or the job I am doing.

127. Tell me about a time when you set a goal in your personal life and achieved it.

Answer:

The interviewer can see that you excel at setting goals in your professional life, but he or she also wants to know that you are consistent in your life and capable of setting goals outside of the office as well. Use an example such as making a goal to eat more healthily or to drink more water and discuss what steps you outlined to achieve your goal, the process of taking action, and the final results as well.

As an example:

Obtaining my accounting certificate was a goal I had set for myself and achieved it. I had wanted to for several years and finally made the decision to do it. For a few years I was very busy and had no extra time nor money to study between family and work. This made me lack motivation. When I ended up having a little extra money one year I decided that it was finally time to accomplish the goal. I set a goal for having it completed by end of spring. Then I researched into the best organization to get certified through based off of what I could afford, studied during my lunch breaks and late at night before I went to bed, and set a test date. I took the test and passed on my first try.

128. What is your greatest goal in your career?

Answer:

Have a very specific goal of something you want to achieve in your career in mind and be sure that it's something the position clearly puts you in line to accomplish. Offer the goal as well as your plans to get there and emphasize clear ways in which this position will be an opportunity to work toward the goal.

As an example:

My career goal is to be a Finance Director by the age of 40. I believe that I can achieve this goal by continuing to move up the ladder, prove myself as a great leader, share my knowledge and work hard. I plan on absorbing as much knowledge as I can these coming years and focusing on my goal while also continuing personal professional development that will prepare me for executive management roles.

129. Tell me about a time when you achieved a goal.

Answer:

Start out with how you set the goal, and why you chose it. Then, take the interviewer through the process of outlining the goal, taking steps to achieve it, the outcome, and finally, how you felt after achieving it or recognition you received. The most important part of this question includes the planning and implementation of strategies, so focus most of your time on explaining these aspects. However, the preliminary decisions and end results are also important, so make sure to include them as well.

As an example:

I was able to completely revamp the filing system in the office I work in. The filing system we used was old and outdated and many of the paper items could be switched to electronic. I met with the business owner of the office I managed and laid out the project. She gave me permission to pursue it. I researched retention schedules for all of the paper items we had and was able to properly dispose of many items. The rest I scanned and filed electronically and had made all new files for any incoming paper items we would receive from then on out. The project was a success and reduced the clutter and allowed everyone to easily and quickly access most items electronically from their desks.

130. What areas of your work would you still like to improve in? What are your plans to do this?

Answer:

While you may not want the interviewer to focus on things you could improve on, it's important to be self-aware of your own growth opportunities. More importantly, you can impress an interviewer by having specific goals and actions outlined in order to facilitate your growth, even if your area of improvement is something as simple as increasing sales or finding new ways to create greater efficiency.

As an example:

I believe I can improve on my ability to say no when need be. I tend to take on additional tasks to easily or offer a helping hand to quickly when I have my own work to do. I am very much interested in teamwork and the success of others and I am working on being able to tell people "no" more often and not extend myself farther than I should. I am getting better and focusing on finishing what needs to be done first then going back and offering my help to others when I have the time to do so.

9

Creativity

Leadership

Teamwork

Deadlines and Time Management

Dedication and Attitude

Personality

Decision Making

Goals

Creative Questions

Customer Service

Background and Experience

Business Skills and Knowledge

Communication

Job Searching and Scheduling

Knowledge of the Company

131. Tell me about your favorite book or newspaper.

Answer:

The interviewer will look at your answer to this question in order to determine your ability to analyze and review critically. Additionally, try to choose something that is on a topic related to your field or that embodies a theme important to your work, and be able to explain how it relates. Stay away from controversial subject matter, such as politics or religion.

As an example:

I enjoy psychology related material seeing as I am in the field of human resources. I find it interested to read about what makes people "tick" and why people are the way they are since I work with people all day, every day. Of course, not everything I read can be applied to my every day job, and every person I come across during the course of a work day is different, I still find it interesting to dive into what doctors have learned about the way the human mind works. Alternatively, maybe a tech related thing like I subscribe to a couple of tech magazines and blogs about coding. Being in IT exposed me to coding and I find it very interesting and like to keep up on new trends. In my spare time I like to code at home and work on fun projects so I enjoy anything tech and coding related.

132. If you could be rich or famous, which would you choose?

Answer:

This question speaks to your ability to think creatively, but your answer may also give great insight to your character. If you answer rich, your interviewer may interpret that you are self-confident and don't seek approval from others, and that you like to be rewarded for your work. If you choose famous, your interviewer may gather that you like to be well-known and to deal with people, and to have the platform to deliver your message to others. Either way, it's important to back up your answer with sound reasoning.

As an example:
Good question and I would say rich so I can have what I need to provide my family with a great life and also donate to several charities and help others as much as I can, sharing the wealth.

133. If you could trade places with anyone for a week, who would it be and why?

Answer:
This question is largely designed to test your ability to think on your feet, and to come up with a reasonable answer to an outside the box question. Whoever you choose, explain your answer in a logical manner, and offer specific professional reasons that led you to choose the individual.

As an example:
At my job, I would want to trade places with a new employee, since I have worked at my employer for so long. I'd like to see what goes through their head as a new person walking in nowadays, what questions they have, what concerns they have, and what they are passionate about so I can better help them succeed and make positive changes where necessary throughout the organization.

134. What would you say if I told you that just from glancing over your resume, I can already see three spelling mistakes?

Answer:

Clearly, your resume should be absolutely spotless - and you should be confident that it is. If your interviewer tries to make you second-guess yourself here, remain calm and poised and assert with a polite smile that you would be quite surprised as you are positive that your resume is error-free.

As an example:

I would say that I am positive the resume is free of errors. I would also thank you for pointing it out to me and double check for accuracy anyway, to be sure I am putting my best foot forward.

135. Tell me about your worldview.

Answer:

This question is designed to offer insight into your personality, so be aware of how the interviewer will interpret your answer. Speak openly and directly and try to incorporate your own job skills into your outlook on life. For example, discuss your beliefs on the ways that hard work and dedication can always bring success, or in how learning new things is one of life's greatest gifts. It's okay to expand into general life principles here but try to keep your thoughts related to the professional field as well.

As an example:

I'd say my worldview is one of hope and optimism, the value of the journey (not just the outcome), and that everyone is capable of achieving greatness. This is true for both personal and work life, in the way that if human beings have a goal that they want to achieve and they do their best they will be sure to learn a lot of valuable lessons along the way. Sometimes life may take us off course and we will travel down different roads than intended, but as long as we are taking time to make positive impacts along the way, learn as much as we can, and value the road we are on and the interactions we have with people we meet, then we are already successful.

136. What is the biggest mistake someone could make in an interview?

Answer:

The biggest mistake during an interview is if you are caught off guard and allow yourself to shut down and have the rest of the interview go downhill as a result. You should be able to portray the fact that you are able to remain on your toes and if you are caught off guard, that you are able to quickly recover. Other common mistakes include not having questions prepared when the interviewer asks if you have questions, arriving late, dressing inappropriate for the setting, showing you did not research the position you applied for, or asking about job benefits at an awkward time during the hiring process.

As an example:

During an interview it may be easy for some candidates to be caught off guard by a question and not know how to answer. This can happen to many people but it can cause a problem if the person doesn't know how to control their emotion and re-focus enough to be able to properly respond. A good method to assure you are able to remain in control of stressful interview situations under pressure is to allow yourself opportunity to think of your answer before attempting to answer, ask the interviewer for a moment to think of the right answer, and of course, breathing techniques. Researching the company and the role ahead of time also helps you feel more prepared and confident walking in, which sets the tone for the entire interview.

137. If you won $50m lottery, what would you do with the money?

Answer:
While a question such as this may seem out of place in a job interview, it's important to display your creative thinking and your ability to think on the spot. It's also helpful if you choose something admirable, yet believable, to do with the money such as donate the first seventy percent to a charitable cause, and divide the remainder among gifts for friends, family, and of course, yourself.

As an example:
This is an easy answer I would definitely pay off my house, my parents house, set aside funds for my children, donate to many charities I support, and set aside the remainder in savings. I may buy something reasonably priced for myself as a little treat, that I wouldn't normally purchase also.

138. Is there ever a time when honesty isn't appropriate in the workplace?

Answer:
This may be a difficult question, but the only time that honesty isn't appropriate in the workplace is perhaps when you're feeling anger or another emotion that is best kept to yourself. If this is the case, explain simply that it is best to put some

Creative Questions

thoughts aside, and clarify that the process of keeping some thoughts quiet is often enough to smooth over any unsettled emotions, thus eliminating the problem

As an example:

There may be situations where in the case of a disagreement at work you may be feeling a little angry or other negative emotions, to take a step back and stop to word your answer properly. If you are indeed angry it would not necessarily be a lie to say something like "I am feeling a little upset.. or disappointed" and allow yourself time to reflect on the situation and come back to work on a solution as well.

139. If you could travel anywhere in the world, where would it be?

Answer:

This question is meant to allow you to be creative - so go ahead and stretch your thoughts to come up with a unique answer. However, be sure to keep your answer professionally-minded. For example, choose somewhere rich with culture or that would expose you to a new experience, rather than going on an expensive cruise through the Bahamas.

As an example:

I would find a large museum I haven't been to and bring my family for a nice weekend trip to visit the museum a couple of days in a row. We would take time to appreciate each display and visit local restaurants and shops we have not tried before.

140. What would I find in your refrigerator right now?

Answer:

An interviewer may ask a creative question such as this in order to discern your ability to answer unexpected questions calmly, or, to try to gain some insight into your personality. For example, candidates with a refrigerator full of junk food or take-out may be more likely to be under stress or have health issues, while a candidate with a balanced refrigerator full of nutritious staples may be more likely to lead a balanced mental life, as well.

As an example:

Plenty of water and iced tea, mixed with some non-caffeine sodas for fun without the caffeine! A lot of yogurts because I love the flavor without it being unhealthy. Cold fruits like grapes are always in stock, and string cheese because it's fun, tasty, and healthy!

141. If you could play any sport professionally, what would it be and what aspect draws you to it?

Answer:

Even if you don't know much about professional sports, this question might be a great opportunity to highlight some of your greatest professional working skills. For example, you may choose to play professional basketball, because you admire the teamwork and coordination that goes into creating a solid play. Or, you may choose to play professional tennis, because you consider yourself to be a go-getter with a solid work ethic and great dedication to perfecting your craft. Explain your choice simply to the interviewer without elaborating on drawn-out sports metaphors and be sure to point out specific areas or skills in which you excel.

facebook.com/vibrantpublishers

As an example:
> *I would be a professional bowler because it's a fun hobby that takes a lot of skill and practice. You are able to work individually as well as be on teams. You can be successful and win tournaments for money without having to deal with the celebrity" aspect since it is a much less commonly-watched sport.*

142. Who were the presidential and vice-presidential candidates in the 2008 elections?

Answer:

These types of questions may be thrown out there not necessarily to see if you know the correct answer, but rather to throw you off and catch you off guard and see how well you handle stress. A good answer will be either the correct answer of course, or if you don't know the answer, find a way to word it to where you don't just say "I don't know." The interviewers are looking at your personality and creativity in how you respond to pressure.

As an example:
> *That's a good question. I don't recall off the top of my head who the president was in 2008. At that time, I was just entering college and while I followed politics here and there, I was mostly focused on studying and passing the next days exams. I am sure right when I leave here today, the answer will enter my head!"*

143. Explain X task in a few short sentences as you would to a second-grader.

Answer:

An interviewer may ask you to break down a normal job task that you would complete in a manner that a child could understand, in part to test your knowledge of the task's inner workings - but in larger part, to test your ability to explain a process in simple, basic terms. While you and your coworkers may be able to converse using highly technical language, being able to simplify a process is an important skill for any employee to have.

As an example:

If I were to explain how to use Microsoft Word to compose a letter, I would suggest they grab a pen and paper for notes. I would show them where to access the software on their computer, how to start a new document, and tell them to properly label and save it before they begin their work. I would encourage them to save their work often throughout the time it takes them to compile the letter so they don't lose any work. I would show them how I type on the computer and compose a short sentence, and then ask them to practice for me so I can give them feedback. I would ask them every so often if they have questions. I would show them basic features and then tell them they can follow up with me if they have further questions or run into problems when they first attempt a letter on their own.

144. If you could compare yourself to any animal, what would it be?

Answer:

Many interviewers ask this question, and it's not to determine which character traits you think you embody - instead, the interviewer wants to see that you can think outside the box, and that you're able to reason your way through any situation. Regardless of what animal you answer, be sure that you provide a thorough reason for your choice.

As an example:

I believe I would be close to a cat. The reason being is that I am versatile, love to work with others and be active, while also enjoying alone time and rest. Cats have a fine balance. They also are intelligent however you are able to teach them new tricks. If you treat a cat nicely, you get a great pet in return. Similar to how I feel in the workplace, if I am heard and provided the tools to succeed, I will produce amazing product and have great loyalty to the company.

145. Who is your hero?

Answer:

Your hero may be your mother or father, an old professor, someone successful in your field, or perhaps even Wonder Woman - but keep your reasoning for your choice professional and be prepared to offer a logical train of thought. Choose someone who embodies values that are important in your chosen career field and answer the question with a smile and sense of passion.

As an example:

> My hero is my mother. She went through hard times but as a child I never would have known. She did a great job at remaining in control in front of those she was supposed to be taking care of (me) and making me feel calm and secure and happy. She knew who she could go to for help when she needed to in terms of other adults and when she had done all she could herself and still needed assistance she did utilize help to get back on her feet and then take it from there. She knew her limits and knew her resources. In work life, it's important to make sure your employees feel safe and happy and have the tools they need to succeed and you always make them feel at ease, while still knowing when the appropriate time comes for you to seek out help and resources to protect or grow your business.

146. Who would play you in the movie about your life?

Answer:

> As with many creative questions that challenge an interviewee to think outside the box, the answer to this question is not as important as how you answer it. Choose a professional, and relatively non-controversial actor or actress, and then be prepared to offer specific reasoning for your choice, employing important skills or traits you possess.

As an example:

> I would say Lucille Ball would play my character (I Love Lucy). She was funny, unique and quirky, and also lovable, confident and a good problem solver.

Creative Questions

147. Name five people, alive or dead, that would be at your ideal dinner party?

Answer:
Smile and sound excited at the opportunity to think outside the box when asked this question, even if it seems to come from left field. Choose dynamic, inspiring individuals who you could truly learn from, and explain what each of them would have to offer to the conversation. Don't forget to include yourself, and to talk about what you would bring to the conversation as well!

As an example:
Myself, Lucille Ball, Abraham Lincoln, Martin Luther King Jr, and George Washington. I would want to ask each of them about their lives during the times they were living in, ask about their childhoods, ask about what they dreamt to be when they were a child and how it compared to what direction their lives actually took, and ask them what advice they'd give todays generation. Admirable women and men in politics, civil rights movements, and breaking gender barriers would all be interesting people to talk with.

This page is intentionally left blank

10

Creativity

Leadership

Teamwork

Deadlines and Time Management

Dedication and Attitude

Personality

Decision Making

Goals

Creative Questions

Customer Service

Background and Experience

Business Skills and Knowledge

Communication

Job Searching and Scheduling

Knowledge of the Company

148. What is customer service?

Answer:

Customer service can be many things - and the most important consideration in this question is that you have a creative answer. Demonstrate your ability to think outside the box by offering a confident answer that goes past a basic definition, and that shows you have truly considered your own individual view of what it means to take care of your customers. The thoughtful consideration you hold for customers will speak for itself.

As an example:

Customer Service is basically any interaction you have with other people during the course of a work day. If you are working in customer service it's simple – you answer the phone, take payments, solve problems. If you work in HR, your customers may be the employees you serve. If you work in sales, your customers may be the people you sell to. Customer Service is show you work with others, your attitude, and your problem-solving abilities. It is wanting to always provide the best service possible, in any capacity you can, to whomever you encounter while at work.

149. Tell me about a time when you went out of your way for a customer.

Answer:

It's important that you offer an example of a time you truly went out of your way - be careful not to confuse something that felt like a big effort on your part, with something your employer would expect you to do anyway. Offer an example of the customer's problems, what you did to solve it, and the way the customer responded after you took care of the situation.

As an example:

I was working with a new client on a large construction job. The client was ready to go with their job and then fell on financial hardship. I wanted to be sure to help the client out so I worked out a payment plan where they did not have to pay for it all upfront. I had them sign a contract noting that I adjusted the payment plan and that it was a one-time situation so they were aware if they used us again in the future it may be payment up front again. The new client was appreciative and the project was completed. We were able to maintain a long-standing relationship with the client and ended up getting more work from them down the road as well as good reviews and increased visibility within the community as a result of word spreading.

150. How do you gain confidence from customers?

Answer:

This is a very open-ended question that allows you to show your customer service skills to the interviewer. There are many possible answers, and it is best to choose something that you've had great experience with, such as "by handling situations with transparency," "offering rewards," or "focusing on great communication." Offer specific examples of successes you've had.

As an example:

Open communication is always good in gaining customer confidence. Instead of just giving any answer just for the sake of providing an answer, I am sure to let the customer know if I don't have an immediate answer to their question and assure them that I will get the right answer and get back with them. Then, I make sure to follow through. Without communication and follow through you will lose trust and they will take their business elsewhere. The customer appreciates honesty and the time you take in delivering them the right answer and the best service.

151. Tell me about a time when a customer was upset or agitated - how did you handle the situation?

Answer:

Similarly, to handling a dispute with another employee, the most important part to answering this question is to first set up the scenario, offer a step-by-step guide to your particular conflict resolution style, and end by describing the way the conflict was resolved. Be sure that in answering questions about your own conflict resolution style, that you emphasize the importance of open communication and understanding from both parties, as well as a willingness to reach a compromise or other solution.

As an example:

Customers who are upset just want to be heard. It is important to listen. I had a customer call when I worked in a billing call center, complaining that she felt she was being charged too much on her monthly bill. She was already agitated when she called and I quickly realized that the more I tried to talk, the more upset she got. I took the time to listen and allow her to fully explain the situation. It became apparent to me that she had not been keeping up to date with the notices that were sent out explaining that there were rate increases. I informed her of the rate increase and waived the first month rate increase, then sent her the notices via e-mail for her to review. I called her the next day to follow up and see if she had any questions.

152. When can you make an exception for a customer?

Answer:

Exceptions for customers can generally be made when in accordance with company policy or when directed by a supervisor. Display an understanding of the types of situations in which an exception should be considered, such as when a customer has endured a particular hardship, had a complication with an order, or at a request.

As an example:

Typically, there are protocols and policies in place to assure that operations are running smoothly and that all customers are being treated fairly while still making sure the company is profitable and not being taken advantage of. There may be times when a customer has an unusual or unexpected hardship that makes it difficult for them to keep up on their payments, and in these situations an extension should be given as a one time courtesy. If the issue continues into the next month, I review the policy manual to see if there is anything else that can be offered and if not, I go to the supervisor for assistance and guidance. At that point it is typically up to the supervisor to make the next call.

153. What would you do in a situation where you were needed by both a customer and your boss?

Answer:

While both your customer and your boss have different needs of you and are very important to your success as a worker, it is always best to try to attend to your customer first - however, the key is explaining to your boss why you are needed urgently by the customer, and then to assure your boss that you will attend to his or her needs as soon as possible (unless it's absolutely an urgent matter).

As an example:

The customer always comes first, and bosses know this most of the time. In situations where a boss may request your assistance at the same time as a customer, it's easy to approach the boss to see what it is they need, get the information, and explain to them that you will be jumping on that task as soon as you are finished assisting the customer. The customer is your source of business and you need to be sure they are taken care of in a timely manner.

154. What is the most important aspect of customer service?

Answer:

While many people would simply state that customer satisfaction is the most important aspect of customer service, it's important to be able to elaborate on other important techniques in customer service situations. Explain why customer service is such a key part of business and be sure to expand on the aspect that you deem to be the most important in a way that is reasoned and well-thought out.

As an example:

The most important aspect of customer service is being genuine. If you do not have a product that genuinely helps the customer, or you are not genuine in your delivery of customer service, the company will fail. Having the ability to enjoy delivering the best customer service and being excited about helping the customer makes the customer also feel excited to do business with you and they feel confident they are being taken care of. Having a pleasant attitude sets the tone for any conversation with a customer and being sure to follow through and do your job to the best of your ability makes the customer feel confident in your services.

155. Is it best to create low or high expectations for a customer?

Answer:

You may answer this question either way (after, of course, determining that the company does not have a clear opinion on the matter). However, no matter which way you answer the question, you must display a thorough thought process, and very clear reasoning for the option you chose. Offer pros and cons of each and include the ultimate point that tips the scale in favor of your chosen answer.

As an example:

It's good to create high expectations from the beginning of any relationship with a newcustomer. This shows you have confidence and makes the customer excited to be on the journey with you. While creating such high expectations though, you should be sure to communicate realistic processes and timeframes so the customer knows that while you are their best choice and they will be glad they chose your company, that things don't happen overnight and a certain level of patience and understanding will need to be had by the customer while they wait for their product to be delivered. Be sure to let them know the wait will be worth it, because you are the best! High expectations, creating excitement, and open communication so they know what to expect, are all important.

This page is intentionally left blank

11

Creativity

Leadership

Teamwork

Deadlines and Time Management

Dedication and Attitude

Personality

Decision Making

Goals

Creative Questions

Customer Service

Background and Experience

Business Skills and Knowledge

Communication

Job Searching and Scheduling

Knowledge of the Company

156. Why did you choose your college major?

Answer:

It's important to display interest in your work, and if your major is related to your current field, it will be simple for you to relate the two. Perhaps you even knew while in college that you wanted to do a job similar to this position, and so you chose the major so as to receive the education and training you needed to succeed. If your major doesn't relate clearly, it's still important to express a sense of passion for your choice, and to specify the importance of pursuing something that matters to you - which is how you made the decision to come to your current career field instead.

As an example:

I chose my major in art history because I was always fascinated by art throughout different time periods. During college I began reading many books and spending a lot of time in libraries where I found several books on my major. I ended up enjoying libraries and discovering new books and enjoyed helping others find books, which is why I decided I would like to work as a librarian. Through my college major I ended up finding my career passion. I am able to work in a setting I love, have access to help many people discover new books and share my love for art history at the same time.

157. Tell me about your college experience.

Answer:

It's best to keep this answer positive - don't focus on parties, pizza, or procrastinating. Instead, offer a general summary of the benefits you received in college, followed by an anecdote of a favorite professor or course that opened up your way of thinking about the field you're in. This is a great opportunity for you to show your passion for your career, make sure to answer enthusiastically and confidently.

As an example:
College definitely helped prepare me for how it feels to have to live on a budget and manage time wisely. I juggled a full course load and a part time job. I was often tired and questioned whether or not I should keep going. I did graduate and was glad I did. All of the times I was too tired to keep going I pushed myself because I knew I could do it and that the ultimate outcome would be worth it. I met many different people from different backgrounds with different perspectives that I had not known before, which was eye opening. I also got some doses of reality thrown in when I had a professor tell me that business management wouldn't be all about "climbing the ladder" and running the show, and I would have to bewilling to work my way up and even then, I'd need to pitch in and get my hands dirty at work sometimes to show employees I was a team player. He had a good way of keeping things real and I appreciated that.

158. What is the most unique thing about yourself that you would bring to this position?

Answer:
This question is often asked as a close to an interview, and it gives you a final chance to highlight your best qualities to the employer. Treat the question like a sort of review, and explain why your specific mix of education, experience, and passions will be the ideal combination for the employer. Remain confident but humble and keep your answer to about two minutes.

As an example:

I believe I have the ability to handle stress pretty well and motivate others during difficult times. While I am able to take things seriously and see the gravity of certain situations, I am also able to maintain composure, hold calm under pressure, and keep others positive. I can typically help keep people grounded and think more clearly and stay motivated to not veer off course even in the face of adversity.

159. How did your last job stand up to your previous expectations of it?

Answer:

While it's okay to discuss what you learned if you expected too much out of a previous job, it's best to keep this question away from negative statements or portrayals. Focus your answer around what your previous job did hold that you had expected, and how much you enjoyed those aspects of the position.

As an example:

I had not expected to be as involved with financial reporting as I was. With that said, I quickly learned that financial reporting was a big part of the job and I had not realized it. I was willing to learn and it helped me to see the big picture and ended up helping me to be more prepared for a management role later down the road.

160. How did you become interested in this field?

Answer:

This is the chance for you to show your passion for your career - and the interviewer will be assured that you are a great candidate if it's obvious that you enjoy your job. You can include a brief anecdote here in order to make your interest personal but be sure that it is brief. Offer specific names of mentors or professors who aided in your discovery and make it clear that you love what you do.

As an example:
I chose the field of engineering because I have always had an interest in how things work and how things are put together. I got in to civil engineering when I had attempted to build a couple of generators at home just for fun during college and realized I was not the best at working with my hands but still was great at putting a plan together. I had talked with a neighbor of mine who was a retired civil engineer who told me all about how he was in the utility industry for many years and oversaw plans for new water mains and was involved heavil yin the building of entire new cities. This piqued my interest and I switched over from mechanical to civil engineering and it is been a fulfilling career with something different everyday.

161. What was the greatest thing you learned while in school?

Answer:
By offering a lesson you learned outside of the classroom, you can show the interviewer your capacity for creativity, learning, and reflection. The practical lessons you learned in the classroom are certainly invaluable in their own right and may pertain closely to the position but showing the mastery of a concept that you had to learn on your own will highlight your growth potential.

As an example:
I learned a great deal in how to prioritize. While juggling different classes and a part time job I often had instances where I had to choose what subject to study, what test to study for, what schedule I'd pick

up at work. *This helped me prepare for my career because I am now better at being able to make a plan of action and decide what needs to be done now and what can wait. I learned that taking care of yourself and maintaining your health and keeping positive attitude and getting plenty of sleep when you can will also help you have more energy and focus more throughout the day.*

162. Tell me about a time when you had to learn a different skill set for a new position.

Answer:

Use a specific example to describe what you had to learn and how you set about outlining goals and tasks for yourself. It's important to show that you mastered the skill largely from your dedication to learning it, and because of the systematic approach you took to developing and honing your individual education. Additionally, draw connections between the skill you learned and the new position, and show how well prepared you are for the job.

As an example:

In my last position my supervisor wanted me to use mail merge for a mass flyer mailing we were doing. I had never used it and didn't know the first thing about it. I looked up a tutorial online and watched the whole thing, then practiced a little. I knew of a coworker who used it often and was an expert in mail merge so I asked her to come on over when she had a free minute and walk me through it in person a couple of times then I practiced in front of her. After a couple of mistakes and trial/error I was able to successfully print 500 flyers with addresses that had been added via mail merge.

163. Tell me about a person who has been a great influence in your career.

Answer:

It's important to make this answer easy to relate to - your story should remind the interviewer of the person who was most influential in his or her own career. Explain what you learned from this person and why they inspired you, and how you hope to model them later in your career with future successes.

As an example:
I had a boss many years ago who I could tell was very protective of me and not necessarily confident in my ability to assert myself in certain settings. He was constantly worried I would be taken advantage of in work settings or people wouldn't take me seriously because I was young. I reminded him much of his eldest child so I think that's why he treated me a bit different. While at first it was a bit of a put off to think he may not have had confidence in my abilities, I understood where he was coming from and worked very hard to prove myself to him. I showed him I was knowledgeable, a hared worker, a team player, and most importantly, assertive enough to be able to handle myself without him having to worry himself over me. The team ended up having a great deal of respect for me and I became a lead worker very quickly. I changed his perception of young people in the workplace and he grew to respect me differently as well. I hope that nowadays I make him proud with my accomplishments and I learned a lot from him and heeded some of the advice he had given me.

164. What would this person tell me about you?

Answer:

Most importantly, if this person is one of your references - they had better know who you are! There are all too many horror stories of professors or past employers being called for a reference, and not being able to recall when they knew you or why you were remarkable, which doesn't send a very positive message to potential employers. This person should remember you as being enthusiastic, passionate, and motivated to learn and succeed.

As an example:

They would say that I am a force to be reckoned with. I am well rounded and able to mesh with any type of person, compassionate about helping others and delivering the best possible service, and a very hard worker. They would say that once given an opportunity, I would not let anyone down.

165. What is the most productive time of day for you?

Answer:

This is a trick question - you should be equally productive all day! While it's normal to become extra motivated for certain projects, and also true that some tasks will require additional work, be sure to emphasize to the interviewer that working diligently throughout the entirety of the day comes naturally to you.

As an example:

I believe I am productive throughout the day. Naturally there may be certain times of day where I may need a little extra spark of energy such as right after a heavy meal at lunch, or other times, but I am able to quickly re-motivate myself with a quick walk or turning some music on and getting down to work.

166. What was the most responsibility you were given at your previous job?

Answer:
This question provides you with an opportunity to elaborate on responsibilities that may or may not be on your resume. For instance, your resume may not have allowed room to discuss individual projects you worked on that were really outside the scope of your job responsibilities, but you can tell the interviewer here about the additional work you did and how it translated into new skills and a richer career experience for you.

As an example:
I was handed the responsibility of organizing the annual employee holiday dinner for five hundred employees and guests. I had a full work load already and limited time to put the event together. I learned that I am capable of pulling off a large event in a short amount of time. I gathered support from other available employees and chose a venue, catering company, decorations and fun ice breakers. I was a bit out of my comfort zone in the beginning and felt overwhelmed, but with a little help and a lot of organization and time management, I was able to pull off the event successfully.

167. Do you believe you were compensated fairly at your last job?

Answer:

Remember to stay positive, and to avoid making negative comments about your previous employer. If you were not compensated fairly, simply state that you believe your qualities and experience were outside the compensation limitations of the old job, and that you're looking forward to an opportunity that is more in line with the place you're at in your career.

As an example:

I believe the pay could have been a little higher in comparison with other agencies however I understand the financial situation the company was in and they did the best they could. What they lacked in pay they made up for in terms of support and work culture. I am looking forward to moving my career forward still having great support and work culture and adding in a higher pay rate.

168. Tell me about a time when you received feedback on your work and enacted it.

Answer:

Try to give an example of feedback your received early in your career, and the steps you took to incorporate it with your work. The most important part of this question is to display the way you learned from the feedback, as well as your willingness to accept suggestions from your superiors. Be sure to offer reflection and understanding of how the feedback helped your work to improve.

As an example:

At my first job as a secretary, my boss told me that I was not asking for help enough. At first this confused me being new to the workforce I thought that it was good if I show I know what I am doing and need little help. I realized that I had made some mistakes in work or was a little behind on certain tasks and that was in fact due to the fact that I wasn't asking enough questions. Because I didn't ask for help, I tried figuring things out on my own and it took longer to complete a task than if I had just asked the boss for a quick answer. She went on to explain to me that while it was good for me to be decisive and figure things out on my own, that when I felt overwhelmed or behind on a task, that I should let her know I was having issues so she could work on a plan to help me improve. After a while I realized that if I tried something on my own and it didn't work, that it was always best to ask for assistance. In the long run it helped me to pick up the pace, complete tasks in a more timely and efficient manner, and open lines between communication with myself and my boss.

169. **Tell me about a time when you received feedback on your work that you did not agree with, or thought was unfair. How did you handle it?**

Answer:

When explaining that you did not agree with particular feedback or felt it was unfair, you'll need to justify tactfully why the feedback was inaccurate. Then, explain how you communicated directly with the person who offered the feedback, and, most importantly, how you listened to their response, analyzed it, and then came to a mutual agreement.

As an example:

> *I was told that I was taking too long to make decisions. I disagreed with this and once I opened up a conversation with the supervisor, I realized that they did not understand everything I was considering while making decisions and why I felt it was important to take my time. On the other hand, I did not realize that the tasks at hand had the urgency they did. Both the supervisor and myself realized we had not been communicating effectively and we made sure to have a meeting before all new projects to allow time for making a plan of action that worked for both of us.*

170. What was your favorite job, and why?

Answer:

It's best if your favorite job relates to the position you're currently applying for, as you can then easily draw connections between why you enjoyed that job and why you are interested in the current position. Additionally, it is extremely important to explain why you've qualified the particular job as your favorite, and what aspects of it you would look for in another job, so that the interviewer can determine whether or not you are a good fit.

As an example:

> *My favorite job was the first one I had in sales. While it was challenging because I was new to the field, it was also the job that really peaked my interest in being in sales and allowed for a lot of trial and error, and I met many people who gave me great advice.*

171. Tell me about an opportunity that your last position did not allow you to achieve.

Answer:

Stay focused on the positive and be understanding of the limitations of your previous position. Give a specific example of a goal or career objective that you were not able to achieve, but rather than expressing disappointment over the missed opportunity, discuss the ways you're looking forward to the chance to grow in a new position.

As an example:

My last company was pretty small and there was only so much room for growth. I want to ultimately grow in to an executive management role, and at my last organization, department supervisor was as high as I could go. While I was able to assist the business owner and fill in for him while he was out of the office, I ultimately was unable to grow past department supervisor. I am thankful for the experience which helped me prepare for more responsibility and higher-level positions within larger organizations.

172. Tell me about the worst boss you ever had.

Answer:

It's important to keep this answer brief, and positively focused. While you may offer a couple of short, critical assessments of your boss, focus on the things you learned from working with such an individual, and remain sympathetic to challenges the boss may have faced.

As an example:

The worst boss I can think of was one who lacked communication skills. They tended to explain things briefly and in only a way they would understand and did not take a lot of opportunity to explain things differently or answer questions employees would ask. It tended to be a bit frustrating to not feel like you were able to approach the boss for questions and assistance. I understand the boss was extremely busy and may have just assumed that you understood the directive the first time. I tended to do my best to try different methods of approach and pose questions in different ways that would allow the boss to answer the question in a different manner and explain the task more thoroughly.

12

Creativity

Leadership

Teamwork

Deadlines and Time Management

Dedication and Attitude

Personality

Decision Making

Goals

Creative Questions

Customer Service

Background and Experience

Business Skills and Knowledge

Communication

Job Searching and Scheduling

Knowledge of the Company

173. What is the best way for a company to advertise?

Answer:

If you're going for a position in any career other than marketing, this question is probably intended to demonstrate your ability to think critically and to provide reflective support for your answers. As such, the particular method you choose is not so important as why you've chosen it. For example, word of mouth advertising is important because customers will inherently trust the source, and social media advertising is important as it reaches new customers quickly and cheaply.

As an example:

Social media is the way to go nowadays since it reaches so many people and is so easy to do. I believe asking for feedback and testimonials from satisfied customers is a great way to advertise in social media. Putting out social media advertisements of great reviews by real customers give your company credibility and sparks interest for more customers to contact you and inquire about your service.

174. Is it better to gain a new customer or to keep an old one?

Answer:

In almost every case, it is better to keep an old customer, and it's important that you are able to articulate why this is. First, new customers generally cost companies more than retaining old ones does, and new customers are more likely to switch to a different company. Additionally, keeping old customers is a great way to provide a stable backbone for the company, as well as to also gain new customers as they are likely to recommend your company to friends.

As an example:

Keeping old customers is best. By maintaining a current customer and focusing on customer satisfaction, you are keeping a customer you already know will be paying for your services. Additionally, if the customer is satisfied, they will be likely to refer you to others as well, and you will gain more customers in the long run.

175. What is the best way to win clients from competitors?

Answer:

There are many schools of thought on the best way to win clients from competitors, and unless you know that your interviewer adheres to a specific thought or practice, it's best to keep this question general. Rather than using absolute language, focus on the benefits of one or two strategies and show a clear, critical understanding of how these ways can succeed in a practical application.

As an example:

The best way to win a client from a competitor is to offer a free trial period, sample, or something along those lines. Instead of just talk about why you are better, prove it to them. It is good to not be too pushy and know when to back off if the potential customer gets too irritated or seems like they are loyal to the competing company. Perhaps in these situations add them to an ongoing list of people you would like to follow up on, and politely reach out to see how things are going. You may just catch them on a day they had a bad experience with their current service.

176. How do you feel about companies monitoring internet usage?

Answer:

Generally speaking, most companies will monitor some degree of internet usage over their employees - and during an interview is not the best time to rebel against this practice. Instead, focus on positive aspects such as the way it can lead to increased productivity for some employees who may be easily lost in the world of resourceful information available to them.

As an example:

Nowadays the internet is just a part of life. There may be times where employees misuse or abuse the internet access at work. It may be on purpose or may be by stumbling on something by accident like a news link they want to read more on when they were supposed to be working on an important project. In either case while it may not make sense for employers to monitor every second of every day or get upset about an employee making a purchase or checking their e-mail during their break, it is good for the company to occasionally monitor to assure their employees are utilizing their time and resources appropriately. In most instances if an employee is informed they need to cut back on internet usage, they will understand and oblige.

177. What is your first impression of our company?

Answer:

Obviously, this should be a positive answer! Pick out a couple key components of the company's message or goals that you especially identify with or that pertain to your experience and discuss why you believe these missions are so important.

As an example:
> *I really like the mission statement of your company. I have done my research and believe that my values align with the company values and I have seen positive reviews from employees as well. I have had a positive interaction today since I arrived as well; everyone seems pleasant and welcoming.*

178. Tell me about your personal philosophy on business.

Answer:
> Your personal philosophy on business should be well-thought out, and in line with the missions and objectives of the company. Stay focused on positive aspects such as the service it can provide, and the lessons people gain in business, and offer insight as to where your philosophy has come from.

As an example:
> *My personal philosophy on business is that it's all about the people. Having good people in place and taking care of them, offering them the tools and support to do their jobs, allowing a good balance of work and personal life, and motivating them will make them better at providing services to the customers. For the people who are customers it's all about making sure their needs are met to the best of the company's ability and treat them with respect.*

179. What's most important in a business model: sales, customer service, marketing, management, etc.?

Answer:
> For many positions, it may be a good strategy to tailor this answer to the type of field you're working in, and to explain why that aspect of business is key. However, by explaining

that each aspect is integral to the function as a whole, you can display a greater sense of business savvy to the interviewer and may stand out in his or her mind as a particularly aware candidate.

As an example:

I believe customer service is key. If you do not have good customer service, you don't maintain current or obtain new customers, and then there's no business at all. While all of these components are important and work together, the customer service portion is most important.

180. How do you keep up with news and emerging trends in the field?

Answer:

The interviewer wants to see that you are aware of what's currently going on in your field. It is important that your education does not stop after college, and the most successful candidates will have a list of resources they regularly turn to already in place, so that they may stay aware and engaged in developing trends.

As an example:

For the field I am in which is IT, I subscribe to tech magazines and am a member of a couple of different tech groups. I often go on forums and discuss new software kinks and bounce ideas off of fellow professionals, as well as practice my skill in my spare time. I am constantly finding new solutions to existing problems and am always ready to solve any new problems that come up. As often as I can, I attend workshops and seminars as they come up.

181. Would you have a problem adhering to company policies on social media?

Answer:

Social media concerns in the workplace have become a greater issue, and many companies now outline policies for the use of social media. Interviewers will want to be assured that you won't have a problem adhering to company standards, and that you will maintain a consistent, professional image both in the office and online.

As an example:

I would not have any problem with social media policies. The only time I would use social media during a work day is during circumstances where it's part of my job, or during my lunch break.

182. Tell me about one of the greatest problems facing X industry today.

Answer:

If you're involved in your career field and spend time on your own studying trends and new developments, you should be able to display an awareness of both problems and potential solutions coming up in the industry. Research some of the latest news before heading into the interview and be prepared to discuss current events thoroughly.

As an example:

One of the biggest problems in the sales arena today is the constantly changing consumer behaviors. It seems just as we have consumers pegged down and can predict their next purchase, things change. This is due to the changing markets, economy, constant addition to product lines, new companies joining the markets every day, and ever changing buyin software. This morning I read an article on a new app that makes it easier for you to trade in your used vehicle same day all online. This will change the strategy for how in person car dealerships handle their trade ins. They will need to come up with creative solutions to match or better that app now. This is just one example of how the market and todays technology is shaping consumer behavior, and we must keep up with it.

183. What do you think it takes to be successful in our company?

Answer:

Research the company prior to the interview. Be aware of the company's mission and main objectives, as well as some of the biggest names in the company, and also keep in mind how they achieved success. Keep your answer focused on specific objectives you could reach in order to help the company achieve its goals.

As an example:

After reviewing your website and reading the Fortune 500 articles about your company, I can see that technology is an important part of your success. It seems you are always on top of the latest software and find creative ways to use it to improve your processes. In order to be successful here I would be on top of learning all of your current software and take an active role in finding new ways to move forward utilizing technology

Business Skills and Knowledge

184. What is your favorite part of working in this career field?

Answer:

This question is an opportunity to discuss some of your favorite aspects of the job, and to highlight why you are a great candidate for the particular position. Choose elements of the work you enjoy that are related to what you would do if hired for the position. Remember to remain enthusiastic and excited for the opportunities you could attain in the job.

As an example:

I enjoy working in the healthcare industry because I was born to help people. It is challenging and rewarding at the same time. I am constantly intrigued with how ever changing the healthcare industry is and how new technology helps doctors and nurses to help more people.

185. What do you see happening to your career in the next 10 years?

Answer:

If you're plugged in to what's happening in your career now and are making an effort to stay abreast of emerging trends in your field, you should be able to offer the interviewer several predictions as to where your career or field may be heading. This insight and level of awareness shows a level of dedication and interest that is important to employers.

As an example:

I started out in administrative work and always enjoyed composing letters and creating flyers and presentations. I volunteered often for these types of projects in my free time. I once thought of myself as being a career administrative professional and quickly realized that not only did I enjoy marketing, I was also good at it. I am studying to obtain my marketing degree and see myself becoming a marketing director ten years from now.

13

Creativity

Leadership

Teamwork

Deadlines and Time Management

Dedication and Attitude

Personality

Decision Making

Goals

Creative Questions

Customer Service

Background and Experience

Business Skills and Knowledge

Communication

Job Searching and Scheduling

Knowledge of the Company

186. Describe a time when you communicated a difficult or complicated idea to a co-worker.

Answer:

Start by explaining the idea briefly to the interviewer, and then give an overview of why it was necessary to break it down further to the coworker. Finally, explain the idea in succinct steps, so the interviewer can see your communication abilities and skill in simplification.

As an example:

I had the idea of a new job scheduling system and needed to present it to the team. I had limited resources and we had not obtained the necessary software yet, so what I did was type up a brief overview of the idea and add main bullet points with images and screen shots of the software from the internet and compiled it into a PowerPoint presentation. I attempted to think of all potential questions that may come up during the meeting and different perspectives so I would be ready to answer questions and present it in a way that would appeal to everyone. I included a list of pros and cons, to include solutions to each con that may come up as well so the team understood I had thought out and was well prepared.

187. What situations do you find it difficult to communicate in?

Answer:

Even great communicators will often find particular situations that are more difficult to communicate effectively in, so don't be afraid to answer this question honestly. Be sure to explain why the particular situation you name is difficult for you and try to choose an uncommon answer such as language barrier or in time of hardship, rather than a situation such as speaking to someone of higher authority.

As an example:

It can sometimes be difficult to communicate effectively when delivering bad news. It is easy to become stressed, or worried about how the person will react. It is important to not attempt to communicate until you feel prepared. Be ready to listen instead of just talk, answer questions you have the answers to, and offer a sense of empathy for what the person is thinking or feeling. Above all it's important to communicate openly and confidently, so the person feels comfortable and has confidence in you or the situation.

188. What are the key components of good communication?

Answer:

Some of the components of good communication include an environment that is free from distractions, feedback from the listener, and revision or clarification from the speaker when necessary. Refer to basic communication models where necessary and offer to go through a role-play sample with the interviewer in order to show your skills.

As an example:

I find it best to be sure to make eye contact and avoid distractions such as the phone or computer while having a serious conversation. Knowing it's ok to ask for clarification is important so there are not any instances of misunderstandings. Reflective listening is a great tool in any communication, where you show the person you were listening to them by repeating back certain things they said when appropriate (For example "I hear you saying you need more support with this project. Let's work on how we can fix it and get you the support you need.

189. Tell me about a time when you solved a problem through communication.

Answer:

Solving problems through communication is key in the business world, so choose a specific situation from your previous job in which you navigated a messy situation by communicating effectively through the conflict. Explain the basis of the situation, as well as the communication steps you took, and end with a discussion of why communicating through the problem was so important to its resolution.

As an example:

My department was having too many misunderstandings due to lack of in person communication and only speaking through e-mail. We never checked our e-mail at the same time and were never on the same page. We continued to overlap on work and tasks were not evenly distributed, with many tasks falling through the cracks. Additionally, there were instances where directives were not clear via e-mail. I requested our department make time for at least bi-weekly department meetings to make sure we were all on the same page and allow time without distraction to address each other and provide updates on department projects. This time together built comradery among the team and provided an effective way to open more lines of communication.

190. Tell me about a time when you had a dispute with another employee. How did you resolve the situation?

Answer:

Make sure to use a specific instance, and explain step-by-step the scenario, what you did to handle it, and how it was finally resolved. The middle step, how you handled the dispute, is clearly the most definitive - describe the types of communication you used, and how you used compromise to reach a decision. Conflict resolution is an important skill for any employee to have and is one that interviewers will search for to determine both how likely you are to be involved in disputes, and how likely they are to be forced to become involved in the dispute if one arises.

As an example:

When I had a dispute with a coworker I asked if we could talk about the issue. They clearly were not interested at first. I let them have their space and checked back a couple of days later, while gently pushing the fact that I respected them and wanted to put the issue behind us so we can both move forward and work together better. I proposed a few different times to meet to discuss the issue and allowed them to choose the time that worked best for them. This made them feel as though they were in some position of control and had buy in. Once we met, I explained again I wanted to move forward and focused on the positive traits about them and our team working abilities and asked them how they felt we should resolve the issue. I listened intently and offered my input once they were finished. We moved forward and put it behind us after that and were able to effectively communicate better than ever before We were also more comfortable to approach each other with any other issues that arose from then on out.

191. Do you build relationships quickly with people, or take more time to get to know them?

Answer:

Either of these options can display good qualities, so determine which style is more applicable to you. Emphasize the steps you take in relationship-building over the particular style and summarize briefly why this works best for you.

As an example:
I feel I get along with anyone pretty quickly and easily build effective working relationships. I am always careful to not get too comfortable too fast, as certain aspects of any relationship take time to develop. While I may run in to people throughout the course of my career that I just do not mesh with well, I am still able to maintain a professional working relationship and mutual respect with them.

192. Describe a time when you had to work through office politics to solve a problem.

Answer:
Try to focus on the positives in this question, so that you can use the situation to your advantage. Don't portray your previous employer negatively, and instead use a minimal instance (such as paperwork or a single individual), to highlight how you worked through a specific instance resourcefully. Give examples of communication skills or problem-solving you used in order to achieve a resolution.

As an example:
There have been many times where I needed to work my way through the "red tape" that was a part of office procedures in getting approvals for new work permits. Although at times it was very frustrating and time consuming, I understood this was necessary as it took time to review the plans and assure the job was going to be done according to safety and legal protocols. I had a job that needed to be rushed, so I prepared a letter explaining the situation, had a statement from the business owner who the job was for, and had my supervisor contact the signing authority to present my case. I was

sure to include reasons why the project would affect the community negatively if put on hold or if it took too long to build, and how rushing the job would be good for the community and opening that store would have a trickle effect in opening other stores in the same vacant lot. While the job ended up not being done the next day, it was moved up two weeks ahead of the original schedule.

193. Tell me about a time when you persuaded others to take on a difficult task.

Answer:

This question is an opportunity to highlight both your leadership and communication skills. While the specific situation itself is important to offer as background, focus on how you were able to persuade the others, and what tactics worked the best.

As an example:

I had a coworker who was reluctant to help me implement a new filing system. The project was going to be time consuming and difficult. I presented her key points on how the project would benefit herself and the entire department and make her job easier, and told her that ultimately it would be something the boss would look kindly on and an opportunity for her to shine. I motivated her by telling her she had really great ideas and that if she were a part of the project it would help for it to get done faster and more efficiently because of her knowledge and ideas. Making her feel good about herself and feel needed motivated her to help.

194. Tell me about a time when you successfully persuaded a group to accept your proposal.

Answer:
This question is designed to determine your resourcefulness and your communication skills. Explain the ways in which you took into account different perspectives within the group and created a presentation that would be appealing and convincing to all members. Additionally, you can pump up the proposal itself by offering details about it that show how well-executed it was.

As an example:

I was trying to purchase a new invoice software that no one was interested in but me. The reason they were not interested was because they were comfortable in the current software and felt they were too busy to learn a new system. I researched the software I was interested in, put together a bullet point list and handed it out to each department member ahead of a scheduled meeting so they would have time to look at it and bring questions with them, and then showcased the software to the team using screen shots and in depth information on how the software would make their jobs easier. I took a couple of coworkers jobs specifically and pointed out how it would directly impact their jobs and improve their processes. I allowed them time to think about it and do more research on their own before making a decision.

195. Tell me about a time when you had a problem with another person, that, in hindsight, you wished you had handled differently.

Answer:
The key to this question is to show your capabilities of reflection and your learning process. Explain the situation, how you handled it at the time, what the outcome of the situation was, and finally, how you would handle it now. Most importantly, tell the interviewer why you would handle it differently now - did your previous solution create stress on the relationship with the other person, or do you wish that you had stood up more for what you wanted? While you shouldn't elaborate on how poorly you handled the situation before, the most important thing is to show that you've grown and reached a deeper level of understanding as a result of the conflict.

As an example:

Many years ago, I had a coworker who never wanted to listen to anything I said, or any of my ideas. They were very stuck in their ways and reluctant in learning new things. I thought the best thing to do was to just avoid them and let them do their own thing and avoid confrontation. In hindsight I could have done better to understand their perspective and potentially their fear of change, and make better attempts at communicating the need for a new process and assuring them that the new process may have made their job easier and we were all a team and would support each other throughout any change. Over the years my ability to communicate and realize that communication is important for teamwork and ultimately the company, has dramatically improved.

196. Tell me about a time when you negotiated a conflict between other employees.

Answer:

An especially important question for those interviewing for a supervisory role - begin with a specific situation and explain how you communicated effectively to each individual. For example, did you introduce a compromise? Did you make an executive decision? Or, did you perform as a mediator and encourage the employees to reach a conclusion on their own?

As an example:

I had many instances as shop supervisor when I acted as a mediator in a dispute between two employees. There was not one go-to solution that would work for every situation since each employee was different and each situation or dispute was different. I would carefully reflect upon the dispute and make a determination for what needed to be done based off of the facts that I was aware of and the personalities of the involved parties. Most often, having both employees sit down together to discuss with me acting as a witness and mediator was very effective. I made sure to allow each the opportunity to present what happened, their perspective, and then how it made them feel or what they thought the best outcome would be. I was sure to always point out that both could have handled the situation differently to avoid the dispute escalating and pointed out the positive traits about each that I felt would allow them to move forward and work together better. I was always sure to follow up to make sure things were still going smoothly and I always had an open door policy if they ran into issues again.

14

Creativity

Leadership

Teamwork

Deadlines and Time Management

Dedication and Attitude

Personality

Decision Making

Goals

Creative Questions

Customer Service

Background and Experience

Business Skills and Knowledge

Communication

Job Searching and Scheduling

Knowledge of the Company

197. What are the three most important things you're looking for in a position?

Answer:

The top three things you want in a position should be similar to the top three things the employer wants from an employee, so that it is clear that you are well-matched to the job. For example, the employer wants a candidate who is well-qualified for and has practical experience - and you want a position that allows you to use your education and skills to their best applications. The employer wants a candidate who is willing to take on new challenges and develop new systems to increase sales or productivity - and you want a position that pushes you and offers opportunities to develop, create, and lead new initiatives. The employer wants a candidate who will grow into and stay with the company for a long time - and you want a position that offers stability and believes in building a strong team. Research what the employer is looking for beforehand and match your objectives to theirs.

As an example:

The three things I am looking for would be opportunity to apply my skillset to make a positive impact, opportunity for growth and learning new things, and stability in a company with a positive mission.

198. How are you evaluating the companies you're looking to work with?

Answer:

While you may feel uncomfortable exerting your own requirements during the interview, the employer wants to see that you are thinking critically about the companies you're applying with, just as they are critically looking at you. Don't be afraid to specify what your needs from a company are (but do try to make sure they match up well with the company - preferably before you apply there) and show confidence and decisiveness in your answer. The interviewer wants to know that you're the kind of person who knows what they want, and how to get it.

As an example:

I am looking at employee satisfaction, company stability, and type of service the company offers. I want to be sure that I am working at a company with good employee feedback so I know the company takes good care of the people on the front lines making the company succeed. I also want to know the company will be around a while and I can stay and grow with the company. Finally, if I want to work with a company that offers a good service to the community and I feel passionate about going to work each day.

199. Are you comfortable working for _____ salary?

Answer:

If the answer to this question is no, it may be a bit of a deal-breaker in a first interview, as you are unlikely to have much room to negotiate. You can try to leverage a bit by highlighting specific experience you have, and how that makes you qualified for more, but be aware that this is very difficult to navigate at this step of the process. To avoid this situation, be aware of industry standards and, if possible, company standards, prior to your application.

As an example:

I am definitely comfortable with starting out at that pay rate. I am happy for the opportunity and know that I will continue to grow within the company.

200. Why did you choose your last job?

Answer:

In learning what led you to your last job, the interviewer is able to get a feel for the types of things that motivate you. Keep these professionally-focused and remain passionate about the early points of your career, and how excited you were to get started in the field.

As an example:

I chose my last job because it was at a non-profit. The pay was lower than a privately held company, however, I knew that it would be a good experience and they needed the help. My skills and knowledge were a great addition to their company and at the time I was able to live off the pay that I received. It was a great experience and now that time has gone by I am ready to move forward in my career and take it to the next level whether it be in non-profit or not, I would like to be able to elevate my career.

201. How long has it been since your last job and why?

Answer:

Be sure to have an explanation prepared for all gaps in employment, and make sure it's a professional reason. Don't mention difficulties you may have had in finding a job, and instead focus on positive things such as pursuing outside interests or perhaps returning to school for additional education.

As an example:

I held my last job about a year ago. I had a very demanding job with long hours, and was doing well financially, however I took some time off for rest and focus on more family time that I felt I was missing out on. During that time, I took some professional development courses and also re-focused my goals and am ready to get back in to the workforce. I feel refreshed, re-trained and re-focused on the area of my field that I am most interested in pursuing.

202. What other types of jobs have you been looking for?

Answer:

The answer to this question can show the interviewer that you're both on the market and in demand. Mention jobs you've applied for or looked at that are closely related to your field, or similar to the position you're interviewing for. Don't bring up last-ditch efforts that found you applying for a part-time job completely unrelated to your field.

As an example:

Because I am pursuing a marketing career, I am focused on marketing jobs in public sector. I am applying mostly for marketing assistant positions and may also be interested in administrative roles if I am still able to have a hand at marketing. I feel pretty confident in my abilities as a successful marketing assistant so I am doing my best to get my foot in the door in that arena, where I can help a company expand their horizons with new creative marketing strategies.

203. Have you ever been disciplined at work?

Answer:

Hopefully the answer here is no - but if you have been disciplined for something at work though, be absolutely sure that you can explain it thoroughly. Detail what you learned from the situation and reflect on how you grew after the process.

As an example:

I have not been disciplined at work however I did receive some criticism on keeping my supervisor better informed on my progress during major projects. I had a tendency to be in the zone and push forward at my own rate, and get the job done and did not think at the time it was important to keep my supervisor up to date if nothing was going wrong. I thought that if something was going wrong, that would be the time to get my boss involved. After discussion, I learned that the supervisor actually had reports they had to submit to upper management once a week, and they had to include my project and where I was at in the process. Once I learned that, I realized that keeping my boss up to date on my projects, even when everything was going right, was always important.

204. What is your availability like?

Answer:

Your availability should obviously be as open as possible, and any gaps in availability should be explained and accounted for. Avoid asking about vacation or personal days (as well as other benefits) and convey to the interviewer how serious you are about your work.

As an example:

I reviewed the business hours and believe my availability would match what the job requires. While I obviously need time to tend to family and personal matters, I am also willing to work overtime as needed as well in order to support the organization.

205. May I contact your current employer?

Answer:

If possible, it is best to allow an interviewer to contact your current employer as a reference. However, if it's important that your employer is not contacted, explain your reason tactfully, such as you just started job searching and you haven't had the opportunity yet to inform them that you are looking for other employment. Be careful of this reasoning though, as employers may wonder if you'll start shopping for something better while employed with them as well.

As an example:

I don't mind at all if you contact my current employer. I would prefer if you were to wait until a contingent offer is made and allow me time to speak with my employer first, out of respect for them so they are not blind sided though. While they were aware that I may eventually leave to grow my career, they will be understandably immediately concerned with filling my position since I play such an important part of the organization. I'd like to be able to speak with them first before they receive a phone call.

206. Do you have any valuable contacts you could bring to our business?

Answer:

It's great if you can bring knowledge, references, or other contacts that your new employer may be able to network with. However, be sure that you aren't offering up any of your previous employer's clients, or in any way violating contractual agreements.

As an example:

I do have some great contacts at other agencies who work with the same software I work with in the accounting field. We have been able to troubleshoot and problem solve together over the years and they share great new ideas with me that help me with things that come up. I'd definitely have much support. I also have a few people who are business owners that can share with your management team any insight they have with how to handle employee issues and new business trends.

207. How soon would you be available to start working?

Answer:

While you want to be sure that you're available to start as soon as possible if the company is interested in hiring you, if you still have another job, be sure to give them at least two weeks' notice. Though your new employer may be anxious for you to start, they will want to hire a worker whom they can respect for giving adequate notice, so that they won't have to worry if you'll eventually leave them in the lurch.

As an example:

While I am eager and excited to begin working with you, I would prefer to give a two week notice to my current employer, out of respect. This will allow time for tying up loose ends and allow me to help them transition during and after my departure.

208. Why would your last employer say that you left?

Answer:

The key to this question is that your employer's answer must be the same as your own answer about why you left. For instance, if you've told your employer that you left to find a position with greater opportunities for career advancement, your employer had better not say that you were let go for missing too many days of work. Honesty is key in your job application process.

As an example:

I believe my last employer would say I left for growth opportunities. While they were sad to see me go, I know they were happy with the time I spent there, and I appreciate of the knowledge I gained while working there.

209. How long have you been actively looking for a job?

Answer:

It's best if you haven't been actively looking for a job for very long, as a long period of time may make the interviewer wonder why no one else has hired you. If it has been awhile, make sure to explain why, and keep it positive. Perhaps you haven't come across many opportunities that provide you with enough of a challenge or that are adequately matched to someone of your education and experience.

As an example:
> I haven't actually been looking for a specific amount of time. I typically only look at job ads if someone sends me something they feel I'd be good at or interested in, as I was not in a hurry to leave my last employer. I saw this job ad and was excited about it so applied for it. It seems like a great opportunity and I feel I would be a good fit. I couldn't pass up on the opportunity to interview and the chance to further my career with your company.

210. When don't you show up to work?

Answer:
> Clearly, the only time acceptable to miss work is for a real emergency or when you're truly sick - so don't start bringing up times now that you plan to miss work due to vacations or family birthdays. Alternatively, you can tell the interviewer how dedicated to your work you are, and how you always strive to be fully present and to put in the same amount of work every time you come in, even when you're feeling slightly under the weather.

As an example:
> Typically, it takes a lot for me to miss work. I will go to work if I have the sniffles I am not one to call in sick because I sneezed or have a slight headache. At the same time, I do not want to get anyone else sick so if I feel truly under the weather, I am sure to stay home. Additionally, of course if there were to be a family emergency that would warrant a sick day, I would give my supervisor ample notice as soon as I found out the need for it. I am good at keeping my boss informed. I also let the boss know of any urgent tasks that may need to be addressed should I expect to miss an entire day so nothing falls

too far behind and there is complete transparency.

211. Have you ever been told by your supervisor to leave work for the day? If so, why?

Answer:

The response to this question will most likely be no, however, if there ever was an instance you were sent home for the day whether it be because you were too sick for work, were having a bad day or being insubordinate, try to word it in a way where you project you understood the reason and have since worked on improving.

As an example:

I have only been sent home once and that was when I was very sick for almost a week. I missed two days of work and was falling behind on my workload. I felt good enough to go to work on the third day and didn't want to fall farther behind. I didn't a fever and felt good enough to show up so I did, but within a couple of hours immediately felt drained, tired, and it was clear that I was not as well as I thought. The boss had asked me when I got there if I was sure I was ok to be at work and I said yes. A couple of hours later she ended up telling me to just go home since it was becoming increasingly difficult to focus with the congestion and weakness I was feeling. I went home and was glad I did. I slept and returned the next day. Nowadays I am better at being sure to take care of myself first and be sure I am good enough to go to work, since health comes first.

212. What is your attendance record like?

Answer:

Be sure to answer this question honestly, but ideally you will have already put in the work to back up the fact that you rarely miss days or arrive late. However, if there are gaps in your attendance, explain them briefly with appropriate reasons, and make sure to emphasize your dedication to your work, and reliability.

As an example:

My attendance record is pretty good. I can't say I have perfect attendance because I am human and have gotten sick enough a couple of times where I needed to call in sick, or had certain appointments that were only available during the same hours I worked. Other than that, I am consistent in showing up to work every day and on time. During rare occurrences of running a few minutes late, I made sure to all and let my boss know, and then even made up for it during lunch or end of day with the bosses' permission.

213. Where did you hear about this position?

Answer:

This may seem like a simple question, but the answer can actually speak volumes about you. If you were referred by a friend or another employee who works for the company, this is a great chance to mention your connection (if the person is in good standing!). However, if you heard about it from somewhere like a career fair or a work placement agency, you may want to focus on how pleased you were to come across such a wonderful opportunity.

As an example:

I heard about the position when a friend of mine sent it to me. She thought it looked interesting and had heard good things about the company. I don't typically care too much about job ads however when I read this one I was excited and very interested and didn't want to pass up the opportunity to apply.

214. Tell me anything else you'd like me to know when making a hiring decision.

Answer:

This is a great opportunity for you to give a final sell of yourself to the interviewer - use this time to remind the interviewer of why you are qualified for the position, and what you can bring to the company that no one else can. Express your excitement for the opportunity to work with a company pursuing X mission.

As an example:

If you hire me you will not be disappointed. I am excited at the opportunity and eager to be able to help your company grow. My skillset and experience seem to match the position perfectly. I'm excited at the prospect of joining the team and seeing how I can "bring solutions to the community" like your company mission says!

This page is intentionally left blank

15

Creativity

Leadership

Teamwork

Deadlines and Time Management

Dedication and Attitude

Personality

Decision Making

Goals

Creative Questions

Customer Service

Background and Experience

Business Skills and Knowledge

Communication

Job Searching and Scheduling

Knowledge of the Company

215. Why would your skills be a good match with X objective of our company?

Answer:

If you've researched the company before the interview, answering this question should be no problem. Determine several of the company's main objectives and explain how specific skills that you have are conducive to them. Also, think about ways that your experience and skills can translate to helping the company expand upon these objectives, and to reach further goals. If your old company had a similar objective, give a specific example of how you helped the company to meet it.

As an example:

I researched your company and saw that you are constantly finding creative ways to leverage new technology to improve your processes. I know one of your objectives is to deliver the best service with the most cost-efficient manner. I am very tech savvy and would be able to help you fast track any new project or software implementation you want to pursue in order to move the company forward. I also saw that you are looking to expand your territories. With my background in marketing and public speaking, and my open and down to earth personality, I would be great at creating marketing material and pitching it to new groups of people. I am very interested in growing with your company.

216. What do you think this job entails?

Answer:

Make sure you've researched the position well before heading into the interview. Read any and all job descriptions you can find (at best, directly from the employer's website or job posting), and make note of key duties, responsibilities, and experience required. Few things are less impressive to an interviewer than a candidate who has no idea what sort of job they're actually being interviewed for.

As an example:
I read the job description and actually brought a copy of it with me. I feel comfortable with all of the job duties listed. I have a couple of questions about the job; and those would be what does a typical day look like and are there opportunities for extra projects as time allows?

217. Is there anything else about the job or company you'd like to know?

Answer:
If you have learned about the company beforehand, this is a great opportunity to show that you put in the effort to study before the interview. Ask questions about the company's mission in relation to current industry trends, and engage the interviewer in interesting, relevant conversation. Additionally, clear up anything else you need to know about the specific position before leaving - so that if the interviewer calls with an offer, you'll be prepared to answer.

As an example:
In researching the company I saw that you are looking to expand your security services from private practice doctor offices to county hospitals. Do you have any specific hospitals you are working on obtaining contracts in so far? How many hospitals or how big of an expansion are you looking in to? What is your vision or plan for the company for the next five years? Finally, what is your company culture like and what do you think your employees would say about working here?

218. Are you the best candidate for this position?

Answer:

Yes! Offer specific details about what makes you qualified for this position and be sure to discuss (and show) your unbridled passion and enthusiasm for the new opportunity, the job, and the company.

As an example:

I am most definitely the best candidate for this position. I would be the most dedicated, hardest worker. I truly understand what it means to be number one in the construction industry and would love to be able to work with your company and bring my skills and ideas to the table, while being able to learn new techniques and learn what's made you so successful. I would love to grow with the company and stay for many years to come.

219. How did you prepare for this interview?

Answer:

The key part of this question is to make sure that you have prepared! Be sure that you've researched the company, their objectives, and their services prior to the interview, and know as much about the specific position as you possibly can. It's also helpful to learn about the company's history and key players in the current organization.

As an example:

In doing my research I found that you were formed in 1975 by John Smith and have grown from 20 employees to 400. I know your mission statement aligns with my values perfectly, and you have a great reputation within the community. I read the job description and the company background, then planned my commute and parking. I am excited at the opportunity to meet with you today.

220. If you were hired here, what would you do on your first day?

Answer:
While many people will answer this question in a boring fashion, going through the standard first day procedures, this question is actually a great chance for you to show the interviewer why you will make a great hire. In addition to things like going through training or orientation, emphasize how much you would enjoy meeting your supervisors and coworkers, or how you would spend a lot of the day asking questions and taking in all of your new surroundings.

As an example:
My first day I would probably be very excited just to be here! I would take as many notes as possible during orientation and process in, gather all necessary forms and benefit information, get a tour of the building, be sure to say hello to my new team mates, ask the team what their most important project is they are working on right now just to get a sense of what I am walking in to and start thinking of ways I can immediately contribute, and also throw out some fun things like get a good idea of what type of music they all listen to! It's nice to be able to have an ice breaker and make a fun first impression, while keeping it professional. Before the end of the day I would be sure to ask my trainer or boss what was on the agenda for the second day.

221. Have you viewed our company's website?

Answer:

Clearly, you should have viewed the company's website and done some preliminary research on them before coming to the interview. If for some reason you did not, do not say that you did, as the interviewer may reveal you by asking a specific question about it. If you did look at the company's website, this is an appropriate time to bring up something you saw there that was of particular interest to you, or a value that you especially supported.

As an example:

I did research the company including visiting the company website. The website is where I first saw the mission statement of bringing joy to the community. I immediately felt connected to the company and wanted to learn more. I took time to review job descriptions, departments, history timeline, and employee reviews.

222. How does X experience on your resume relate to this position?

Answer:

Many applicants will have some bit of experience on their resume that does not clearly translate to the specific job in question. However, be prepared to be asked about this type of seemingly-irrelevant experience, and have a response prepared that takes into account similar skill sets or training that the two may share.

As an example:

While I do not have direct experience in using Quickbooks software for invoicing customers, I do have experience with AccountVoice

Knowledge of the Company 193

software, which is very similar. I have utilized AccountVoice for several years and am sure I would be able to learn Quickbooks very quickly.

223. Why do you want this position?

Answer:

Keep this answer focused positively on aspects of this specific job that will allow you to further your skills, offer new experience, or that will be an opportunity for you to do something that you particularly enjoy. Don't tell the interviewer that you've been looking for a job for a long time, or that the pay is very appealing, or you will appear unmotivated and opportunistic.

As an example:

I want this position because it's a great opportunity working for a growing company where I can see myself staying for many years. I feel I have reached the highest potential at my current employer and am seeking growth in a stable organization that has a positive mission. Your company is on trend to continue its growth, has great reviews, and many opportunities to work on larger scale projects in my field. I crave creativity and fast paced environments. I believe with your growing company that is constantly taking on new clients, I would be a huge asset and bring many great ideas to the table.

224. How is your background relevant to this position?

Answer:

Ideally, this should be obvious from your resume. However, in instances where your experience is more loosely-related to the position, make sure that you've researched the job and company well before the interview. That way, you can intelligently relate the experience and skills that you do have, to similar skills that would be needed in the new position. Explain specifically how your skills will translate and use words to describe your background such as "preparation" and "learning." Your prospective position should be described as an "opportunity" and a chance for "growth and development."

As an example:

I believe my background in marketing has helped to prepare me for this public information officer role. I have worked in both marketing and management, and in both positions, I had to find creative ways to reach many people and communicate important updates and events. I am well versed in many methods of marketing from mailings to social media and more and have spoken to large groups of up to 500 people at a time. I would be able to effectively and articulately compile marketing material, deliver it in the best method for each situation, and track responses and make adjustments accordingly.

225. How do you feel about X mission of our company?

Answer:

It's important to have researched the company prior to the interview - and if you've done so, this question won't catch you off guard. The best answer is one that is simple, to the point, and shows knowledge of the mission at hand. Offer a few short statements as to why you believe in the mission's importance and note that you would be interested in the chance to work with a company that supports it.

As an example:

The mission of your company resonates deeply with me because you prove that you are company who values people first. Your mission of "people is our mission" proves that above all else you understand that people are what makes your company move, and people are providing servicesto people. Being centered around what matters is a great value to have and proves you are not just about profit. I would love to be a part of an organization with such a positive mission statement.

Index

Human Resource Interview Questions

Creativity

001. Every business faces problems that affect productivity and profitability. Can you share with me a solution you developed for a workplace problem that was unusual or unexpected, and actually led to increased productivity or profitability?

002. Can you describe how you analyzed a workplace problem you have faced, and how your analysis led to the solution?

003. There are times when customers are unhappy with your company's product or service and expect a solution that is more than what is normally provided. Can you share a time when you were able to provide a solution to an unusual customer expectation that made both customer and management happy?

004. Describe workplace innovations you have developed on your own initiative.

005. Describe workplace innovations you helped develop as a member of a team.

006. Where do you find ideas?

007. How do you achieve creativity in the workplace?

008. How do you push others to create ideas?

009. Describe your creativity.

Leadership

010. Was there a time you were called upon to reorganize your department? If so, what steps did you take to ensure the reorganization was successful?

011. Tell me about a time when you led a team to successfully complete a project.

012. Describe a time when you played a major leadership role in a special event.

013. How have the people around you responded to your leadership efforts?
014. Describe your strengths as a leader.
015. Describe the greatest weakness in your leadership style.
016. If a group of people in your department were talking about you behind your back, what do you think they would be saying about you?
017. Describe a difficult project that required you to build consensus on a divisive issue.
018. Describe a project or task that required you to develop agreement or cooperation between departments.
019. Describe a situation when you needed to build support within your department for an idea you thought would greatly benefit your company.
020. Would you rather receive more authority or more responsibility at work?
021. What do you do when someone in a group isn't contributing their fair share?
022. Tell me about a time when you made a decision that was outside of your authority.
023. Are you comfortable going to supervisors with disputes?
024. If you had been in charge at your last job, what would you have done differently?
025. Do you believe employers should praise or reward employees for a job well done?
026. What do you believe is the most important quality a leader can have?
027. Tell me about a time when an unforeseen problem arose. How did you handle it?
028. Can you give me an example of a time when you were able to improve X objective at your previous job?
029. Tell me about a time when a supervisor did not provide specific enough direction on a project.
030. Tell me about a time when you were in charge of leading a project.
031. Tell me about a suggestion you made to a former employer that was later implemented.

032. Tell me about a time when you thought of a way something in the workplace could be done more efficiently.
033. Is there a difference between leading and managing people - which is your greater strength?
034. Do you function better in a leadership role, or as a worker on a team?
035. Tell me about a time when you discovered something in the workplace that was disrupting your (or others) productivity - what did you do about it.
036. How do you perform in a job with clearly-defined objectives and goals?
037. How do you perform in a job where you have great decisionmaking power?
038. If you saw another employee doing something dishonest or unethical, what would you do?
039. Tell me about a time when you learned something on your own that later helped in your professional life.
040. Tell me about a time when you developed a project idea at work.
041. Tell me about a time when you took a risk on a project.
042. What would you tell someone who was looking to get into this field?

Teamwork

043. How would you handle a negative coworker?
044. What would you do if you witnessed a coworker surfing the web, reading a book, etc, wasting company time?
045. How do you handle competition among yourself and other employees?
046. When is it okay to socialize with co-workers?
047. Tell me about a time when a major change was made at your last job, and how you handled it.
048. When delegating tasks, how do you choose which tasks go to which team members?
049. Tell me about a time when you had to stand up for something you believed strongly about to coworkers or a supervisor.

050. Tell me about a time when you helped someone finish their work, even though it wasn't "your job."
051. What are the challenges of working on a team? How do you handle this?
052. Do you value diversity in the workplace?
053. How would you handle a situation in which a coworker was not accepting of someone else's diversity?
054. Are you rewarded more from working on a team, or accomplishing a task on your own?

Deadlines and Time Management

055. Tell me about a time when you didn't meet a deadline.
056. How do you eliminate distractions while working?
057. Tell me about a time when you worked in a position with a weekly or monthly quota to meet. How often were you successful?
058. Tell me about a time when you met a tough deadline, and how you were able to complete it.
059. How do you stay organized when you have multiple projects on your plate?
060. How much time during your workday do you spend o n "auto-pilot?"
061. How do you handle deadlines?
062. Tell me about your personal problem-solving process.
063. What sort of things at work can make you stressed?
064. How do you outwardly respond to stress in the workplace? How do you calm yourself down when you are feeling stressed?
065. Are you good at multi-tasking? Give some examples of how you successfully multi-tastk?
066. How many hours per week do you work?
067. How many times per day do you check your email?

www.vibrantpublishers.com

Dedication and Attitude

068. Tell me about a time when you worked additional hours to finish a project.
069. Tell me about a time when your performance exceeded the duties and requirements of your job.
070. What is your driving attitude about work?
071. Do you take work home with you?
072. Describe a typical work day to me.
073. How would you handle not getting a promotion you interview for at your current employer?
074. Are you open to receiving feedback and criticisms on your job performance, and adjusting as necessary?
075. What inspires you?
076. How do you inspire others?

Personality

077. What has been your biggest success?
078. What motivates you?
079. What do you do when you lose motivation?
080. What do you like to do in your free time?
081. What sets you apart from other workers?
082. Why do you feel you are the best candidate for this position?
083. What does it take to be successful?
084. What would be the biggest challenge in this position for you?
085. Would you describe yourself as an introvert or an extrovert?
086. What are some positive character traits that you don't possess?
087. What is the greatest lesson you've ever learned?
088. Have you ever been in a situation where one of your strengths became a weakness in an alternate setting?
089. Who has been the most influential person in your life?
090. Do you consider yourself to be a "detailed" or "big picture" type of person?

091. What is your greatest fear?
092. What sort of challenges do you enjoy?
093. Tell me about a time you were embarrassed. How did you handle it?
094. What is your greatest weakness?
095. What are the three best adjectives to describe you in a work setting?
096. What are the three best adjectives to describe you in your personal life?
097. What type of worker are you?
098. Tell me about your happiest day at work.
099. Tell me about your worst day at work.
100. What are you passionate about?
101. What is the piece of criticism you receive most often?
102. What type of work environment do you succeed the most in?
103. Are you an emotional person?

Decision Making

104. Have you come across any decision-making situations in the past?
105. How will you make decisions under pressure?
106. Do you think it is always important to make ethically correct decisions?
107. Does your emotional maturity play a role in making decisions?
108. Do you think decision making should be done by the manager or by a team?
109. Good business decisions are based on sound empirical evidence. Do you agree with this view?
110. When do you think a team can be involved in decision-making?
111. Do you think decision-making is a form of planning? If yes, what is the similarity between the two?
112. In a financial services company like ours how do you think decisions should be made?
113. What are the steps to be followed in attaining a decision?
114. How do you make decisions?

115. What are the most difficult decisions for you to make?
116. When making a tough decision, how do you gather information?
117. Tell me about a decision you made that did not turn out well.
118. Are you able to make decisions quickly?

Goals

119. Ten years ago, what were your career goals?
120. Tell me about a weakness you used to have, and how you changed it.
121. Tell me about your goal-setting process.
122. Tell me about a time when you solved a problem by creating actionable steps to follow.
123. Where do you see yourself five years from now?
124. When in a position, do you look for opportunities to promote?
125. On a scale of 1 to 10, how successful has your life been?
126. What is your greatest goal in life?
127. Tell me about a time when you set a goal in your personal life and achieved it.
128. What is your greatest goal in your career?
129. Tell me about a time when you achieved a goal.
130. What areas of your work would you still like to improve in? What are your plans to do this?

Creative Questions

131. Tell me about your favorite book or newspaper.
132. If you could be rich or famous, which would you choose?
133. If you could trade places with anyone for a week, who would it be and why?
134. What would you say if I told you that just from glancing over your resume, I can already see three spelling mistakes?
135. Tell me about your worldview.
136. What is the biggest mistake someone could make in an interview?

137. If you won $50m lottery, what would you do with the money?
138. Is there ever a time when honesty isn't appropriate in the workplace?
139. If you could travel anywhere in the world, where would it be?
140. What would I find in your refrigerator right now?
141. If you could play any sport professionally, what would it be and what aspect draws you to it?
142. Who were the presidential and vice-presidential candidates in the 2008 elections?
143. Explain X task in a few short sentences as you would to a second-grader.
144. If you could compare yourself to any animal, what would it be?
145. Who is your hero?
146. Who would play you in the movie about your life?
147. Name five people, alive or dead, that would be at your ideal dinner party?

Customer Service

148. What is customer service?
149. Tell me about a time when you went out of your way for a customer.
150. How do you gain confidence from customers?
151. Tell me about a time when a customer was upset or agitated - how did you handle the situation?
152. When can you make an exception for a customer?
153. What would you do in a situation where you were needed by both a customer and your boss?
154. What is the most important aspect of customer service?
155. Is it best to create low or high expectations for a customer?

Background and Experience

156. Why did you choose your college major?
157. Tell me about your college experience.
158. What is the most unique thing about yourself that you would bring to this position?
159. How did your last job stand up to your previous expectations of it?
160. How did you become interested in this field?
161. What was the greatest thing you learned while in school?
162. Tell me about a time when you had to learn a different skill set for a new position.
163. Tell me about a person who has been a great influence in your career.
164. What would this person tell me about you?
165. What is the most productive time of day for you?
166. What was the most responsibility you were given at your previous job?
167. Do you believe you were compensated fairly at your last job?
168. Tell me about a time when you received feedback on your work and enacted it.
169. Tell me about a time when you received feedback on your work that you did not agree with, or thought was unfair. How did you handle it?
170. What was your favorite job, and why?
171. Tell me about an opportunity that your last position did not allow you to achieve.
172. Tell me about the worst boss you ever had.

Business Skills and Knowledge

173. What is the best way for a company to advertise?
174. Is it better to gain a new customer or to keep an old one?
175. What is the best way to win clients from competitors?
176. How do you feel about companies monitoring internet usage?
177. What is your first impression of our company?

178. Tell me about your personal philosophy on business.
179. What's most important in a business model: sales, customer service, marketing, management, etc.?
180. How do you keep up with news and emerging trends in the field?
181. Would you have a problem adhering to company policies on social media?
182. Tell me about one of the greatest problems facing X industry today.
183. What do you think it takes to be successful in our company?
184. What is your favorite part of working in this career field?
185. What do you see happening to your career in the next 10 years?

Communication

186. Describe a time when you communicated a difficult or complicated idea to a co-worker.
187. What situations do you find it difficult to communicate in?
188. What are the key components of good communication?
189. Tell me about a time when you solved a problem through communication.
190. Tell me about a time when you had a dispute with another employee. How did you resolve the situation?
191. Do you build relationships quickly with people, or take more time to get to know them?
192. Describe a time when you had to work through office politics to solve a problem.
193. Tell me about a time when you persuaded others to take on a difficult task.
194. Tell me about a time when you successfully persuaded a group to accept your proposal.
195. Tell me about a time when you had a problem with another person, that, in hindsight, you wished you had handled differently.
196. Tell me about a time when you negotiated a conflict between other employees.

Job Searching and Scheduling

197. What are the three most important things you're looking for in a position?
198. How are you evaluating the companies you're looking to work with?
199. Are you comfortable working for _____ salary?
200. Why did you choose your last job?
201. How long has it been since your last job and why?
202. What other types of jobs have you been looking for?
203. Have you ever been disciplined at work?
204. What is your availability like?
205. May I contact your current employer?
206. Do you have any valuable contacts you could bring to our business?
207. How soon would you be available to start working?
208. Why would your last employer say that you left?
209. How long have you been actively looking for a job?
210. When don't you show up to work?
211. Have you ever been told by your supervisor to leave work for the day? If so, why?
212. What is your attendance record like?
213. Where did you hear about this position?
214. Tell me anything else you'd like me to know when making a hiring decision.

Knowledge of the Company

215. Why would your skills be a good match with X objective of our company?
216. What do you think this job entails?
217. Is there anything else about the job or company you'd like to know?
218. Are you the best candidate for this position?
219. How did you prepare for this interview?
220. If you were hired here, what would you do on your first day?

221. Have you viewed our company's website?
222. How does X experience on your resume relate to this position?
223. Why do you want this position?
224. How is your background relevant to this position?
225. How do you feel about X mission of our company?

Some of the following titles might also be handy:

1. NET Interview Questions You'll Most Likely Be Asked
2. Access VBA Programming Interview Questions You'll Most Likely Be Asked
3. Adobe ColdFusion Interview Questions You'll Most Likely Be Asked
4. Advanced C++ Interview Questions You'll Most Likely Be Asked
5. Advanced Excel Interview Questions You'll Most Likely Be Asked
6. Advanced JAVA Interview Questions You'll Most Likely Be Asked
7. Advanced SAS Interview Questions You'll Most Likely Be Asked
8. AJAX Interview Questions You'll Most Likely Be Asked
9. Algorithms Interview Questions You'll Most Likely Be Asked
10. Android Development Interview Questions You'll Most Likely Be Asked
11. Ant & Maven Interview Questions You'll Most Likely Be Asked
12. Apache Web Server Interview Questions You'll Most Likely Be Asked
13. Artificial Intelligence Interview Questions You'll Most Likely Be Asked
14. ASP.NET Interview Questions You'll Most Likely Be Asked
15. Automated Software Testing Interview Questions You'll Most Likely Be Asked
16. Base SAS Interview Questions You'll Most Likely Be Asked
17. BEA WebLogic Server Interview Questions You'll Most Likely Be Asked
18. C & C++ Interview Questions You'll Most Likely Be Asked
19. C# Interview Questions You'll Most Likely Be Asked
20. CCNA Interview Questions You'll Most Likely Be Asked
21. Cloud Computing Interview Questions You'll Most Likely Be Asked
22. Computer Architecture Interview Questions You'll Most Likely Be Asked
23. Computer Networks Interview Questions You'll Most Likely Be Asked
24. Core JAVA Interview Questions You'll Most Likely Be Asked
25. Data Structures & Algorithms Interview Questions You'll Most Likely Be Asked
26. EJB 3.0 Interview Questions You'll Most Likely Be Asked
27. Entity Framework Interview Questions You'll Most Likely Be Asked
28. Fedora & RHEL Interview Questions You'll Most Likely Be Asked
29. Hadoop BIG DATA Interview Questions You'll Most Likely Be Asked
30. Hibernate, Spring & Struts Interview Questions You'll Most Likely Be Asked
31. HR Interview Questions You'll Most Likely Be Asked
32. HTML, XHTML and CSS Interview Questions You'll Most Likely Be Asked
33. HTML5 Interview Questions You'll Most Likely Be Asked
34. IBM WebSphere Application Server Interview Questions You'll Most Likely Be Asked
35. iOS SDK Interview Questions You'll Most Likely Be Asked
36. Java / J2EE Design Patterns Interview Questions You'll Most Likely Be Asked
37. Java / J2EE Interview Questions You'll Most Likely Be Asked
38. JavaScript Interview Questions You'll Most Likely Be Asked
39. JavaServer Faces Interview Questions You'll Most Likely Be Asked
40. JDBC Interview Questions You'll Most Likely Be Asked
41. jQuery Interview Questions You'll Most Likely Be Asked
42. JSP-Servlet Interview Questions You'll Most Likely Be Asked
43. JUnit Interview Questions You'll Most Likely Be Asked
44. Leadership Interview Questions You'll Most Likely Be Asked
45. Linux Interview Questions You'll Most Likely Be Asked
46. Linux System Administrator Interview Questions You'll Most Likely Be Asked
47. Mac OS X Lion Interview Questions You'll Most Likely Be Asked
48. Mac OS X Snow Leopard Interview Questions You'll Most Likely Be Asked

facebook.com/vibrantpublishers

Some of the following titles might also be handy:

49. Microsoft Access Interview Questions You'll Most Likely Be Asked
50. Microsoft Powerpoint Interview Questions You'll Most Likely Be Asked
51. Microsoft Word Interview Questions You'll Most Likely Be Asked
52. MySQL Interview Questions You'll Most Likely Be Asked
53. Networking Interview Questions You'll Most Likely Be Asked
54. OOPS Interview Questions You'll Most Likely Be Asked
55. Operating Systems Interview Questions You'll Most Likely Be Asked
56. Oracle Database Administration Interview Questions You'll Most Likely Be Asked
57. Oracle E-Business Suite Interview Questions You'll Most Likely Be Asked
58. ORACLE PL/SQL Interview Questions You'll Most Likely Be Asked
59. Perl Programming Interview Questions You'll Most Likely Be Asked
60. PHP Interview Questions You'll Most Likely Be Asked
61. Python Interview Questions You'll Most Likely Be Asked
62. RESTful JAVA Web Services Interview Questions You'll Most Likely Be Asked
63. SAP HANA Interview Questions You'll Most Likely Be Asked
64. SAS Programming Guidelines Interview Questions You'll Most Likely Be Asked
65. Selenium Testing Tools Interview Questions You'll Most Likely Be Asked
66. Silverlight Interview Questions You'll Most Likely Be Asked
67. Software Repositories Interview Questions You'll Most Likely Be Asked
68. Software Testing Interview Questions You'll Most Likely Be Asked
69. SQL Server Interview Questions You'll Most Likely Be Asked
70. Tomcat Interview Questions You'll Most Likely Be Asked
71. UML Interview Questions You'll Most Likely Be Asked
72. Unix Interview Questions You'll Most Likely Be Asked
73. UNIX Shell Programming Interview Questions You'll Most Likely Be Asked
74. Windows Server 2008 R2 Interview Questions You'll Most Likely Be Asked
75. XLXP, XSLT, XPATH, XFORMS & XQuery Interview Questions You'll Most Likely Be Asked
76. XML Interview Questions You'll Most Likely Be Asked

For complete list visit

www.vibrantpublishers.com

NOTES

Printed in the USA
CPSIA information can be obtained
at www.ICGtesting.com
LVHW010427010624
781837LV00004B/469